CHANGING LAWS

Politics of the Civil Rights Era

JUDY DODGE CUMMINGS

EXPLORE QR CONNECTIONS!

You can use a smartphone or tablet app to scan the QR codes and explore more! Cover up neighboring QR codes to make sure you're scanning the right one. You can find a list of urls on the Resources page.

If the QR code doesn't work, try searching the internet with the Keyword Prompts to find other helpful sources.

civil rights politics

Nomad Press

A division of Nomad Communications

10 9 8 7 6 5 4 3 2 1

This book was manufactured by CGB Printers, North Mankato, Minnesota, United States
October 2020, Job #1010678
ISBN Softcover: 978-1-61930-927-2
ISBN Hardcover: 978-1-61930-924-1

Educational Consultant, Marla Conn

Questions regarding the ordering of this book should be addressed to
Nomad Press
2456 Christian St., White River Junction, VT 05001
www.nomadpress.net

Printed in the United States.

Discover the PASSION and CONVICTION of the 1950s, '60s, and '70s!

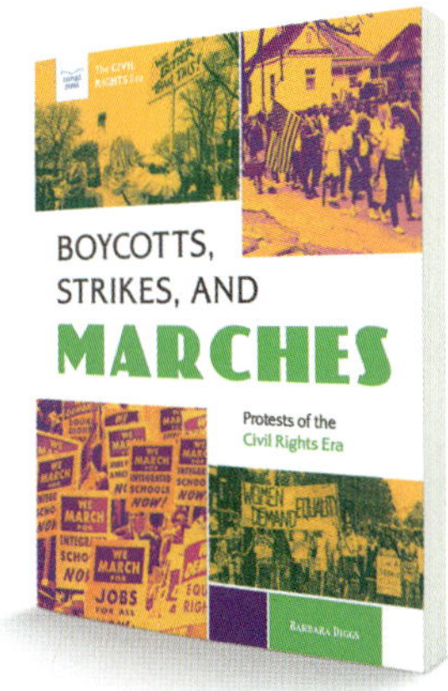

In *Boycotts, Strikes, and Marches: Protests of the Civil Rights Era*, readers 12 through 15 explore five groundbreaking protests that took place during the 1950s, 1960s, and early 1970s. Become immersed in the spirit of the Montgomery bus boycott, the draft card burning protests of the Vietnam War, the Delano grape strike and boycott, the first Gay Pride March, and the Women's Strike for Equality. Middle schoolers also learn about the conditions that prompted these demonstrations and how protest organizers used critical and creative thinking to surmount the challenges they faced to initiate meaningful change.

Sitting In, Standing Up: Leaders of the Civil Rights Era, tells the story of one of the most tumultuous and important eras in American history through the lives of five major figures of the Civil Rights Movement of the 1950s and 1960s: Thurgood Marshall, Fannie Lou Hamer, Martin Luther King Jr., Ella Baker, and John Lewis. The work of these people sparked the passion of a nation and helped change the tide of social injustice in a way that reverberates to this day.

Singing for Equality: Musicians of the Civil Rights Era introduces middle graders to the history of the Civil Rights Movement and explores the vital role that music played in the tumultuous period of American history during the 1950s, '60s, and '70s.

The heart of the Civil Rights Movement beats in the music and musicians of the times, whose work was both an inspiration and a reflection of the changes happening in America and to its people. Bob Dylan, Mavis Staples and the Staple Singers, Nina Simone, Sam Cooke, and James Brown epitomized the passion and commitment shown by those involved in the movement and portrayed the struggles encountered by an entire race of people with gritty beauty and moving calls to action and thought.

TABLE OF

CONTENTS

Le Petit Journal

SUPPLEMENT ILLUSTRÉ

DIMANCHE 7 OCTOBRE 1906

LES « LYNCHAGES » AUX ÉTATS-UNIS

Massacre de nègres à Atlanta (Georgie)

Rioting in the South, 1906

Jim Crow laws make segregation a way of life.

Signing of the 1964 Civil Rights Act

Marching for equal rights, 1963

U.S. President Lyndon B. Johnson signs the 1964 Civil Rights Act as Martin Luther King Jr. and others look on.

Credit: Cecil Stoughton, White House Press Office

INTRODUCTION

THE POLITICAL PATH

The Civil Rights Movement changed lives—it also changed laws. As the dust of the marches, riots, and sit-ins settled, lawmakers at all levels of government were working hard to ensure that the gains made during the Civil Rights Movement were lasting. By making change into law, people hoped to prevent a backslide into the inequalities of the past.

FAST FACTS

WHAT?

The Civil Rights Movement was a struggle for justice and equality by African Americans.

WHY?

African Americans and other groups had long been treated unequally by the law, and the time for change was overdue.

WHEN?

From the mid 1950s to early 1970s

HOW?

The U.S. Supreme Court made decisions that helped level the playing field for African Americans seeking employment, housing, and representation in government.

Vote at age 18, have a fair trial if accused of a crime, attend a decent school, play in a public park, drink from a water fountain, be served in a restaurant—these basic rights of political and social equality are some of the civil rights that Americans are promised. The Fourteenth Amendment to the Constitution forbids any state from discriminating against citizens and denying them "the equal protections of the laws." The U.S. Congress passed this amendment in 1868 as part of a plan to integrate newly freed slaves into society.

However, the U.S. Supreme Court intervened. In a series of decisions in the 1870s and 1880s, the court ruled that only state and local governments, not Congress, could pass laws preventing racial discrimination. This opened the door to Jim Crow laws and decades of racial injustice, including the murder of Emmett Till in 1955.

Word Power!

This book is packed with lots of new vocabulary! Try figuring out the meanings of unfamiliar words using the context and roots of the words. There is a glossary in the back to help you and Word Power check-ins for every chapter.

Meet Emmett

During the summer of 1955, 14-year-old Emmett Till (1941–1955) left his Chicago, Illinois, home and boarded a train. His mother, Mamie Till-Mobley, warned her son to be careful while he was visiting relatives in Money, Mississippi. The South held dangers for a young, Black male.

CIVIL RIGHTS TIMELINE

1954 The U.S. Supreme Court decision *Brown v. Board of Education* rules that segregated schools are unconstitutional.

1957 President Eisenhower sends in federal troops to protect nine Black students as they integrate Central High School in Little Rock, Arkansas.

1960 The support of Black voters helps John F. Kennedy win the presidential election.

On August 24, Till was hanging around the town's general store with his cousins and some other Black teenagers. He was bragging about dating white girls back in Chicago, so the other kids dared him to flirt with Carolyn Bryant (1934–), the white store owner.

At a bus station in Durham, North Carolina, 1940

Credit: Jack Delano

Till took the dare. He entered the store and bought some candy. Just before exiting, he whistled long and low at Carolyn Bryant. His cousin, Simeon Wright (1942–2017), knew Till had crossed an invisible line. "Man, that scared us half to death," said Wright. The three boys raced home and hid in a field, telling no one what Till had done.

Payback came on August 28. Late that night, Carolyn's husband, Roy Bryant (1931–1994), and his brother, J.W. Milam (1919–1980), barged into the house where Till was staying and dragged him from bed. Three days later, Till's body was found in the Tallahatchie River. He had been pistol whipped and shot in the head.

Life Under Jim Crow

As the murder of Emmett Till showed, there were lines in the South that African Americans dared not cross. After the Civil War ended in 1865, a period of reform called Reconstruction gave African Americans hope that these color lines might vanish. After the horrors of slavery, years when Black people had no rights and were considered property of white owners, Reconstruction seemed like the best chance to right past wrongs and create a better future.

June 19, 1964
The Civil Rights Bill is voted in as law to prohibit segregation in public accommodations.

August 6, 1965
President Johnson signs the Voting Rights Act, outlawing discrimination in voting practices.

April 11, 1968
After the assassination of Dr. Martin Luther King Jr., President Johnson pushes Congress into passing the Fair Housing Bill.

November 5, 1968
The election of Richard M. Nixon as president signals a retreat from federal support for major civil rights legislation.

Not only did the South's infrastructure need to be rebuilt after the Civil War, so did society.

By the twentieth century, Jim Crow dominated Southern culture from birth to death. Black babies and white babies were born at separate hospitals. Black students and white students attended separate schools. Dead Blacks and dead whites were embalmed at separate mortuaries and buried in separate cemeteries. There were segregated orphanages, hotels, restaurants, and waiting rooms. Railroad cars, streetcars, steamboats, and ferries separated Blacks and whites on public transportation.

Jim Crow laws were extreme. Blacks and whites drank from separate water fountains and used different Bibles to swear an oath in court. North Carolina demanded that textbooks used by white and Black students be stored separately in the summer. The Red Cross even segregated America's supply of donated blood. Segregation was written into the law and brutally enforced.

During this time, Republicans in Congress passed laws to grant African Americans rights they had long been denied. However, in 1877, the federal government removed troops from the South. Without soldiers to enforce the new laws, white planters, businessmen, and politicians in the Democratic Party used violence and economic influence to regain power. During the next two decades, officials passed state and local laws to separate Blacks and whites throughout public life. This segregation system was called Jim Crow.

THE GAINS OF RECONSTRUCTION

During the Reconstruction era, 1865–1877, Congress ratified three constitutional amendments to safeguard the liberty of African Americans. The Thirteenth Amendment abolished slavery. The Fourteenth Amendment recognized Black people as citizens entitled to equal protection under the law. The Fifteenth Amendment gave Black men the right to vote. For the first time, former slaves could legally marry, purchase land, and own businesses. New schools for African Americans taught grandparents to read alongside their grandchildren. More than 700,000 Southern Black men registered to vote and 2,000 held elected office. For this brief era, racial equality seemed possible.

WHO WAS JIM CROW?

During the 1830s, the white actor Thomas Dartmouth Rice (1808–1860) created a popular minstrel show. He painted his face black and danced and sang. In one of his most popular songs, Rice pretended to be a slow-witted slave named "Jim Crow." By the time minstrel shows went out of fashion, the phrase "Jim Crow" had come to refer to anti-Black laws throughout the south.

Race Riots and Lynch Law

Violence against African Americans was common across the country. These attacks generally took two forms—race riots and lynching. Riots occurred mostly in cities whereas lynching was a rural custom.

The summer of 1919 was labeled "Red Summer." White mobs invaded Black neighborhoods in riots that exploded in 26 cities, including Chicago, Illinois; Nashville, Tennessee; Washington, DC; and Omaha, Nebraska. More than 100 African Americans were killed and thousands were injured and left homeless.

Oklahoma City, Oklahoma, 1939

Credit: Russell Lee

In Atlanta, Georgia, tough economic times combined with politicians looking for someone to blame was the recipe for a race riot in 1906. Atlanta was home to several Black colleges, successful Black-owned businesses, and the largest Black middle class in the country. Well-educated African Americans threatened some white peoples' idea of racial supremacy.

Smoke billowing over Tulsa, Oklahoma, during the 1921 race riots

Credit: Alvin C. Krupnick Co., retrieved from Library of Congress

After the Civil War, Atlanta had developed quickly. The population exploded and competition for jobs increased. Race relations became strained in the overcrowded city. When Democrat Hoke Smith (1855–1931) ran for governor in 1906, he played on this tension. Smith campaigned to end the vote for African Americans in Georgia. He claimed there was an epidemic of Black men assaulting white women. Newspapers stirred tensions with headlines such as "Bold Negro Kisses White Girl's Hand." These accusations were based on rumor or were just plain false, but that did not matter to white readers.

AMERICAN TERRORISM: THE KU KLUX KLAN

The power of the Ku Klux Klan (KKK) has ebbed and flowed for more than a century. This terrorist group was founded after the Civil War. Its members used violence and terror to prevent former slaves from gaining power. The federal government crushed the KKK in the 1880s, but the group rose again during the 1920s following mass immigration from Europe. In that decade, between 2 and 4 million Americans became members of the Klan. The group opposed nonwhites, immigrants, Jews, Catholics, and left-wing politicians. A third wave of Klan activity surged in the 1960s in response to the Civil Rights Movement. In the second decade of the twenty-first century, white supremacy is once again on the rise, fueled by hatred of Muslims, immigrants, and LGBTQ activism. In 2017, there were 42 different Klan groups active in 22 states.

CONNECT

View this map of some of the race riots of the summer of 1919. What were the common factors that caused this violence to erupt?

arcgis race riot map

Le Petit Journal

Le Petit Journal
CHAQUE JOUR — 6 PAGES — 5 CENTIMES
Administration : 61, rue Lafayette

Le Supplément illustré
CHAQUE SEMAINE 5 CENTIMES

5 Centimes SUPPLÉMENT ILLUSTRÉ 5 Centimes

Le Petit Journal Militaire, Maritime, Colonial.... 10 cent.
Le Petit Journal agricole, 5 cent. La Mode du Petit Journal, 10 cent.
Le Petit Journal illustré de La Jeunesse.... 10 cent.
On s'abonne sans frais dans tous les bureaux de poste

ABONNEMENTS

	SIX MOIS	UN AN
SEINE ET SEINE-ET-OISE	2 fr.	3 fr. 50
DÉPARTEMENTS	2 fr.	4 fr. »
ÉTRANGER	2 50	5 fr. »

Les manuscrits ne sont pas rendus

Dix-septième année DIMANCHE 7 OCTOBRE 1906 Numero 829

LES « LYNCHAGES » AUX ÉTATS-UNIS
Massacre de nègres à Atlanta (Georgie)

On September 22, 1906, Atlanta newspapers reported on four alleged sexual assaults on white women by Black men. A mob of angry whites surged through the center of the city, attacking Black people on the streets and destroying Black-owned businesses. When African Americans resisted, the governor called in the militia. Three days later, 26 people were dead and many more were injured.

Lynching was the common form of racial violence in the rural south. A lynching was a public murder of a person suspected of committing a crime. The suspect was not put on trial and usually there was no evidence of guilt—just rumors. A mob of whites would seize the suspect and execute him, usually by hanging or shooting. From 1882 to 1951, at least 3,457 Black Americans were lynched.

The cover of a French magazine depicting the Atlanta race riot

> "No colored man, no matter what his reputation, is safe from lynching if a white woman, no matter what her standing or motive, cares to charge him with insult or assault."
>
> Ida B. Wells (1865–1931), African American journalist

White Southerners justified these murders by claiming white women needed protection from dangerous Black men. In the late nineteenth century, Benjamin Tillman, a governor and senator from South Carolina, said if lynching rapists violated the U.S. Constitution, "then to hell with the Constitution."

> **"I think everybody needed to know what had happened to Emmett Till."**
>
> **Mamie Till-Mobley** (1920–2003) on her decision to have an open casket at her son's funeral

However, historical studies prove that rape was often used as an excuse to justify murdering Black people who dared violate Jim Crow customs. If a Black man tried to vote, testify in court, or have a consensual romantic relationship with a white woman, he risked being accused of rape and lynched. Because the lynch mob often included local sheriffs, judges, and prosecutors, the murderers were rarely punished.

WONDER WHY?

Why were white Southerners determined to keep the races separate?

The Spark

Emmett Till was killed in this racial climate. On September 23, 1955, Roy Bryant and J.W. Milam were tried for Till's murder. Carolyn Bryant testified that Till had grabbed her around the waist and "made ugly remarks" about white women. The all-white jury deliberated for only 15 minutes before returning a verdict of not guilty.

A few weeks after the trial, Roy Bryant and J.W. Milam sold their story to *Look* magazine for $4,000. They bragged to the reporter that they had killed Emmett Till because he seemed unafraid of them.

Carolyn Bryant remained silent about Emmett Till for decades. Then, in 2008, she gave an interview about what really happened in 1955. Bryant said she had lied about Till grabbing her and making sexually crude comments. She said, "Nothing that boy did could ever justify what happened to him."

Wheeler Parker, Till's cousin, does not hold ill-will toward Carolyn Bryant. "I can't hate," he said. "Hate destroys the hater, too. That's a heavy burden to carry."

Vivian Malone, one of the first African Americans to attend University of Alabama, enters Foster Auditorium to register for classes.

Credit: Warren K. Leffler, *U.S. News & World Report* magazine collection

No one served time in prison for Till's murder. However, his death marked a turning point in the struggle for civil rights.

Till's death was different from previous lynchings. His mother, Mamie Till-Mobley, insisted on an open casket at her son's funeral. More than 50,000 people attended the service, and *Jet* magazine ran a story that included a photograph of the boy's beaten and bruised corpse. The nation was horrified.

A Civil Rights Movement had been slowly developing in the South, and Till's brutal murder fueled activists with a grim determination to change society. They united in a movement to defeat Jim Crow.

Making Change

Civil rights activists developed a strategy of nonviolent resistance. Mass marches, boycotts, and sit-ins drew the wrath of Southern whites. The eyes of the world zeroed in on scenes of angry white mobs blocking Black children from entering schools and enraged white men beating activists for attempting to ride buses across state lines.

A civil rights march in Washington, DC, 1963

Credit: Warren K. Leffler

Media coverage of the violence pressured the federal government to take action. However, change was slow and victories hard-won. Local politicians defended Jim Crow at all costs.

Members of Congress were split—many Northern Democrats supported civil rights legislation while Southern Democrats and some Republicans opposed it. Presidents Eisenhower, Kennedy, Johnson, and Nixon worried about alienating Southern white voters and feared violating the Constitution, and so they were slow to lead.

The politics of the Civil Rights Movement was a complicated clash of competing powers. State and local laws collided with the Constitution. Governors brawled with presidents. The U.S. Supreme Court overrode state courts.

In the middle of this power struggle, civil rights activists plodded tirelessly on, determined to achieve equality. School desegregation, the 1964 Civil Rights Act, the 1965 Voting Rights Act, the Fair Housing Act of 1968, and the legacies of several governments were all results of the work done during the Civil Rights Movement.

In this book, we'll take a closer look at the people and processes that made these changes possible.

WONDER WHY?

What about today? Do we need more laws to address inequality? Why?

PROJECT

Does Racial Inequality Exist in Your School?

It can sometimes be hard to recognize racial inequality when it doesn't directly affect you. Take a look at the statistics relating to your own school and see if anything surprised you.

- **Explore racial inequality across the country.** Go to this link to find the database "Miseducation" from ProPublica.

ProPublica miseducation

- **Scroll down to the interactive map** and click on the tabs "Opportunity," "Discipline," "Segregation," and "Achievement Gap."

- **What conclusions can you draw from the information on this map?** Consider the following questions.
  - What questions does this data raise?
  - How do educational opportunities and discipline compare across the states?
  - Is there a relationship between the percent of nonwhite students in a state and the suspension rates of nonwhites compared to white students?

- **Search for your school district in the database.** What information do you discover about your school?

- **Create an annotated map of the schools in your community.** Using the data in the database, illustrate or explain any segregation and educational inequality in your district on the map itself.

- **Share your map with classmates and teachers.** What explanations do people have for the segregation and inequality that exists in your local schools? What solutions do people have for how to improve this problem?

TEXT TO WORLD

Have you ever felt as though your civil rights were being violated? What did you do?

Soldiers from the 101st Airborne Division escort African American students to Central High School in Little Rock, Arkansas, in September 1957, after the governor tried to enforce segregation.

Credit: Photo courtesy National Archives. Operation Arkansas

CHAPTER ONE

SEPARATE IS NOT EQUAL

One September morning in 1950, seven-year-old Linda Brown (1943–2018) clung to her father's hand as they walked to Sumner Elementary School. Only four blocks from Linda's house in Topeka, Kansas, was a school for white children only. Because Linda was Black, she had to travel all the way across town to the school reserved for African Americans.

FAST FACTS

WHAT?

The U.S. Supreme Court case *Brown v. the Board of Education of Topeka* ruled that segregated schools were unconstitutional.

WHY?

Schools for African Americans were consistently worse than schools for white children.

WHEN?

May 17, 1954

HOW?

Through legal arguments, the National Association for the Advancement of Colored People (NAACP) convinced the U.S. Supreme Court that segregated schools created a system of inequality that was damaging to Black children.

Her father, Reverend Oliver Brown, was determined to enroll Linda in Sumner Elementary, the school for white children.

As she waited in the foyer, Linda heard her father's frustration as he spoke with the principal. On the walk home, Linda felt her father's anger in his tight grip on her hand. The principal had refused to let Linda enroll.

The Civil Rights Movement's first target was the South's segregated education system. When activists pried open the doors of Jim Crow schools, they shook the political system from statehouses to the White House.

In February 1951, the National Association for the Advancement of Colored People (NAACP) filed a lawsuit against the Topeka school district. The NAACP attorney argued that segregated schools violated the Fourteenth Amendment to the Constitution. But a three-judge panel ruled in favor of the school district.

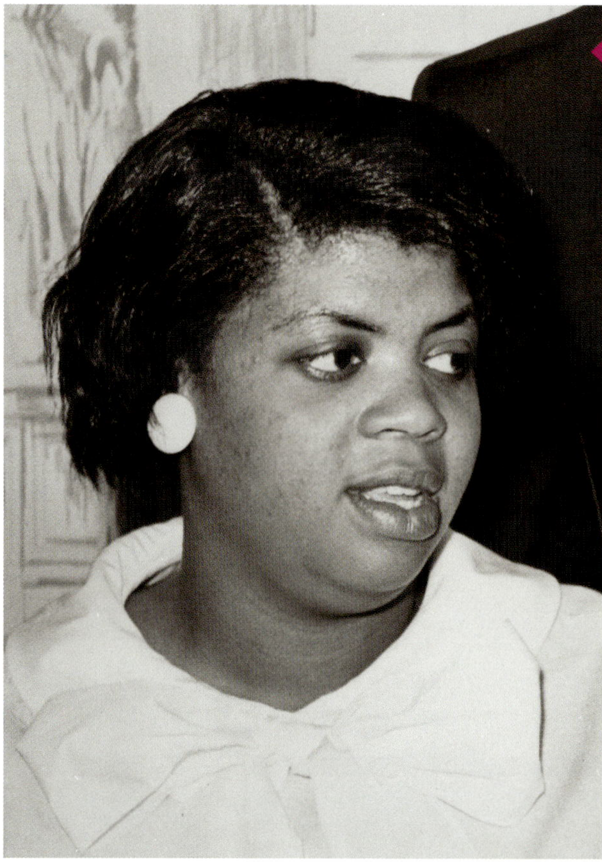

Linda Brown in 1964

Separate But Equal

The stumbling block for African Americans was the 1896 U.S. Supreme Court ruling, *Plessy v. Ferguson*. A Louisiana man named Homer Plessy (1862–1925) refused to sit in the train compartment reserved for Black people, which violated Louisiana's Separate Car Act. Police arrested Plessy.

CIVIL RIGHTS TIMELINE

1896
In *Plessy v. Ferguson*, the U.S. Supreme Court rules that racially segregated schools are legal as long as they are equal.

1954
In *Brown v. Board of Education*, the U.S. Supreme Court overturns the Plessy decision, ruling that racially segregated schools were unconstitutional.

A segregated classroom in Virginia during the 1950s

WONDER WHY?

Have you ever held a belief that was different from what your peers believe? How did others react to you?

Claiming his Fourteenth Amendment rights had been violated, Plessy filed suit in federal court. The case worked its way to the U.S. Supreme Court, where the justices ruled against Plessy. They said segregating citizens by race or color was legal as long as the facilities provided to each race were equal. This "separate but equal" doctrine became the legal foundation for Jim Crow laws everywhere. That's how life was lived for decades.

1956
Southern congressmen write the Southern Manifesto, vowing to fight school desegregation.

1957
Congress passes the Civil Rights Act of 1957, creating a civil rights division in the U.S. Justice Department and a commission to investigate civil rights abuses.

1957
When violence erupts in Little Rock, Arkansas, President Eisenhower sends troops to protect nine Black teenagers attempting to integrate Central High School.

Jump ahead to 1950—Linda Brown's father refused to give up. Thurgood Marshall (1908–1993), the chief lawyer for the NAACP Legal Defense and Education Fund, believed the time had come to challenge *Plessy*. He combined Linda Brown's case with school desegregation cases from four other states. In December 1952, Marshall argued the case called *Brown v. Board of Education* before the U.S. Supreme Court.

Segregation is Inherently Unequal

On May 17, 1954, the justices unanimously overturned *Plessy*, handing Black Americans their first victory of the Civil Rights Movement. The court ruled that segregated schools created feelings of inferiority in the "hearts and minds" of Black children and deprived them of equal educational opportunities. Therefore, segregated schools were "inherently unequal." The court ordered Southern states to desegregate "with all deliberate speed."

African Americans were overjoyed. NAACP Director Roy Wilkins (1901–1981) said, "May 17, 1954, was one of life's sweetest days." *The Pittsburgh Courier*, a Black newspaper, called for a day of prayer and thanksgiving. When Linda Brown's father, Oliver Brown, told her the news, he had tears in his eyes.

"We conclude that, in the field of public education, the doctrine of 'separate but equal' has no place."

Chief Justice Earl Warren (1891 – 1974)

WONDER WHY?

Do you see schools today that have mostly Black or mostly white kids? How do they get this way when segregation is illegal?

Massive Resistance

For Southern whites, the *Brown* decision was a bombshell that sparked a resistance campaign. A White Citizens Council movement arose. Middle- and upper-class whites joined loosely connected local groups that used political action and economic intimidation to block desegregation.

Mississippi had 60,000 White Citizens Council members. When 53 Black residents of Yazoo County, Mississippi, signed a petition asking county schools to desegregate, the council published their names in the newspaper. These people were fired from their jobs, evicted from their homes, and had banks cancel their credit. All 53 petitioners withdrew their signatures—the county's NAACP chapter closed.

Southern state politicians also found ways around desegregation. Prince Edward County, Virginia, simply stopped funding all public education, and North Carolina passed a "pupil placement law." This allowed school districts to use "race neutral" criteria such as family income to assign children to different schools. This was just a ploy to continue racial segregation in North Carolina's schools.

Henry L. Moon, Roy Wilkins, Herbert Hill, and Thurgood Marshall holding a poster against racial bias in Mississippi in 1956

Credit: *New York World-Telegram and the Sun* staff photographer Al Ravenna

Many Southern congressmen rallied Southern whites to fight back. On March 12, 1956, 82 representatives and 19 senators signed the Declaration of Constitutional Principles. Nicknamed the "Southern Manifesto," this statement called *Brown v. Board of Education* "null, void, and of no effect" and urged Southerners to use all lawful means to resist desegregation. A constitutional crisis loomed.

President Eisenhower at a press conference, October 9, 1957. What do you notice about all the people in the room? Why is this important?

Eisenhower's Silence

Americans who looked to President Dwight Eisenhower (1890–1969) for leadership found a man caught between two powerful forces. On one hand, the president believed the rule of law was the foundation of American democracy and *Brown* was the law. But he also believed white Southerners would eventually desegregate and did not want to force change too quickly.

President Eisenhower's own racial views and political ambitions might also have influenced his go-slow approach. He once told U.S. Supreme Court Chief Justice Earl Warren that Southerners were not evil. "All they are concerned about is to see that their sweet little girls are not required to sit in school alongside some big overgrown Negroes." Do you think this is a racist statement? Why or why not?

BETTER THAN NO BILL AT ALL

On September 9, 1957, President Eisenhower signed the Civil Rights Act of 1957, the first civil rights law in 82 years. The law created a civil rights division of the U.S. Justice Department and a commission to investigate civil rights abuses. However, the law did not give the U.S. Attorney General the power to punish people who violated the Fourteenth Amendment. This disappointed civil rights activists. Despite the weakness, Martin Luther King Jr. believed the "present bill is far better than no bill at all."

Eisenhower was running for reelection in 1956. Afraid to push away white voters, he remained silent as Southern resistance grew when the school year began.

On August 30, a mob prevented 12 Black students from entering the white high school in Mansfield, Texas. Posters tacked to the doors showed Black people dangling from nooses. One sign read: "This Negro tried to enter a white school." ("Negro" was a term for Black people that was unacceptable by the late 1960s.) The governor of Texas sent seven tanks, three armored personnel carriers, and 100 jeeps to control violence in Clinton, Tennessee, when Black students tried to enroll at the white high school. Schools had become combat zones.

> "All the nation is watching in shocked horror at men making war upon children . . . and . . . [the president] chooses to stand mute."
>
> **Roy Wilkins**, NAACP director in 1956

A TOUGH JOB

Everett Frederic Morrow (1909–1994) was the first Black adviser to a president. He worked for President Eisenhower from 1954 to 1961. People often mistook Morrow for a butler, and when the president traveled, Morrow had to stay in Black-only hotels. Eisenhower did not seem to understand the injustices Black Americans experienced. In 1958, Morrow arranged for the president to speak at a meeting of Black leaders. Instead of promising to protect Black peoples' rights, Eisenhower told his audience to have "patience" because he did not want to violate the rights of white Americans by forcing them to integrate. When Morrow heard this, he said, "I could feel life draining from me, and I wished I could escape."

President Eisenhower claimed his hands were tied. "Under the law the federal government cannot . . . move into a state until the state is not able to handle the matter." It took a crisis in Little Rock, Arkansas, to force Eisenhower to act.

Soldiers Bar the Schoolhouse Door

The Little Rock, Arkansas, school board picked nine Black teenagers to integrate Central High School in 1957. But before the plan could be implemented, a white supremacist group pressured Governor Orval Faubus (1910–1994) to block it. Faubus was a moderate Republican, but he was running for reelection against a segregationist. Faubus decided that to win reelection, he had to take a strong stand against integration.

The evening of September 2, 1957, Faubus ordered 200 Arkansas National Guard soldiers to circle Central High School. On September 4, the nervous Black teenagers known as the "Little Rock Nine" headed for school. Daisy Bates (1914–1999), the local NAACP leader, led eight of the students, but 16-year-old Elizabeth Eckford (1941–) missed the call for the students to gather. She rode a city bus to school alone.

A crowd of protestors heckled the eight students as they tried to enter Central High School. A line of soldiers blocked their entry, so the students turned around and went home. But when Elizabeth Eckford arrived by herself, she assumed the soldiers were there to protect her.

Orval Faubus, August 20, 1959

A young boy watches white people march in protest of school integration in Little Rock, August 1959.

Eckford felt relieved—until she tried to enter a side door. Two soldiers crossed their rifles. "It was only then," she recalled, "that I realized they were barring me."

A local photographer snapped a photo of Eckford as she left school, and it appeared on the front page of newspapers around the country the next day. Eckford is shown walking to the bus stop wearing a grim expression. On her heels is a white girl, eyes narrowed and mouth twisted in a snarl. This was the face of Jim Crow.

THE UNTIRING DAISY BATES

Daisy Bates's (1914–1999) life was shaped by the struggle for civil rights. Her birth mother was raped and murdered by three white men when Bates was very young. When Bates grew up, she was elected president of the Arkansas NAACP. Bates was targeted because she supported the Little Rock Nine. A rock was thrown through the window of her home, a cross was burned on her lawn, and the newspaper she owned was financially ruined. But Bates never stopped fighting. In an interview she gave at age 75, Bates said, "I'm not too tired to . . . do what I can for the cause I believe in."

On September 20, District Court Judge Ronald Davies ordered Governor Faubus to admit the Black students. Faubus simply removed the National Guard. Technically, he had obeyed the law. But now the Little Rock Nine were at the mercy of the mob.

Eisenhower Sends in Federal Force

As the Little Rock Nine approached school on September 23, they heard the rumble of a mob 1,000 strong. The crowd mistook some Black reporters for students and attacked. During this distraction, the Black students slipped into school through a side entrance and waited in the principal's office. When the crowd discovered the students had gotten past them, its rumble became a roar.

Hundreds of white students walked out of school chanting, "Two, four, six, eight, we ain't gonna integrate." The mayor and school superintendent feared protestors might storm the building, so police sneaked the students out of school and drove them away.

WONDER WHY?

Have you seen protests at your school? What was the topic? Was it nonviolent or did people get angry and violent?

The next day, the Little Rock Nine stayed home, but the protestors returned to the school grounds. Little Rock's mayor sent a telegram to President Eisenhower. "The immediate need for federal troops is urgent . . . . Situation is out of control."

A 1959 rally at the Arkansas state capitol protesting the admission of the Little Rock Nine to Central High School

Credit: John T. Bledsoe, *U.S. News & World Report* magazine collection

"They used to call Arkansas 'the land of opportunity,' and Black people said, 'Opportunity for whom? Today, we can say, 'Opportunity for all,' and Arkansas can be proud of this moment."

Ernest Green (1941 –), one of the Little Rock Nine

This was the invitation Eisenhower needed. According to the Insurrection Act of 1807, if a rebellion in a state prevents U.S. laws from being enforced, the president can empower troops to enforce those laws. By 7 p.m. on September 24, 1,000 federal troops rolled into Little Rock.

New York City Mayor Robert Wagner greets the teenagers who integrated Central High School, 1958.

Credit: *New York World-Telegram and the Sun* staff photographer Walter Albertin

CONNECT

You can see the famous photograph of Elizabeth Eckford and read more about her relationship with the people in the mob at this website. What do you think of Eckford's quote, "True reconciliation can occur only when we honestly acknowledge our painful, but shared, past"?

History Little Rock scream

Eisenhower explained his actions in a televised address. "Mob rule cannot be allowed to override the decisions of our courts," he said. While he praised the majority of Southerners who were "united in their efforts to . . . respect the law," he was silent about the need for racial equality. Eisenhower wanted to uphold the law, not defend civil rights.

The National Guard remained at Central High School for the rest of the school year to protect the Black students. The following year, Governor Faubus closed the city's public schools rather than integrate.

Racial equality was a long way off. As the Eisenhower administration ended, civil rights activists took their struggle beyond the schoolhouse to tackle Jim Crow everywhere.

WONDER WHY?

How would your life be different if the U.S. Supreme Court had not overturned segregation in schools?

PROJECT

Mendez v. Westminster

Nine-year-old Sylvia Mendez (1936–), a Mexican American, won the right to attend an all-white school in California eight years before the *Brown* victory. Create a picture book to tell the story of her role in school desegregation.

- **Write a research question to help you discover how the 1946 case of *Mendez v.* Westminster laid the groundwork for Brown v. Board of Education in 1954.**
- **Using the internet, locate videotaped interviews with Sylvia Mendez and articles about *Mendez v. Westminster*.** What arguments used in the *Mendez* decision would later come up in the *Brown* case?
- **Write and illustrate a nonfiction picture book about Sylvia Mendez's desegregation fight.** A picture book has 500-1,000 words and includes a theme, setting, characters, plot, and a balance of pictures and words suited to young readers.
- **Read your picture book to an audience.** Then lead a discussion about the case.

Word Power!

What vocabulary words did you discover? Can you figure out the meanings of these words? Look in the glossary for help!

deliberate, desegregate, doctrine, economic, heckle, implement, intimidation, manifesto, moderate, neutral, petition, and segregate

CONNECT

Schools are still segregated today, more than 60 years after the *Brown* decision. Watch the video on this link to figure out why.

KQED racially segregated

TEXT TO WORLD

What might your education be like if you went to an all-Black or all-white school?

More than 10,000 people marched down 16th Street NW from All Souls Church to Lafayette Square in Washington, DC, September 22, 1963, following the bombing deaths of four children at a church and the shooting deaths of two other children in Birmingham, Alabama.

Credit: Thomas J. O'Halloran. Courtesy of the Library of Congress (CC BY 2.0)

CHAPTER TWO

NOW IS THE TIME

FAST FACTS

WHAT?
The Civil Rights Act of 1964 banned discrimination on the basis of race, color, religion, or national origin.

WHY?
Without a federal law preventing it, rampant discrimination would continue at all levels of society.

WHEN?
July 2, 1964

HOW?
Because of work done by the Freedom Riders and those who took part in the Children's March, among other protests, the federal government created a new law that would protect the rights of Black Americans.

The presidential election of 1960 was a nail-biter. John F. Kennedy (1917–1963), the Democratic senator from Massachusetts, faced off against Richard Nixon, the Republican vice president. The outcome of the race depended on many things, but high on that list were African American voters.

Both men pursued the Black vote, but most African Americans backed Kennedy. Their support helped him defeat Nixon by less than 1 percent of the national vote. African Americans expected the new president to take a strong stand on civil rights—Kennedy had other plans, however.

THE PHONE CALL

Nixon had a solid civil rights record and African Americans might have voted for him instead of Kennedy except for one phone call. In October 1960, Martin Luther King Jr. was arrested on a trumped-up charge in Georgia and sentenced to six months in a maximum security prison. King's friends asked both Kennedy and Nixon to help free him. Neither candidate wanted to lose support from Southern whites, but Kennedy's aides convinced him to call King's wife. When news of the call leaked to the press, Georgia officials released King from prison. That phone call persuaded Blacks that Kennedy was committed to racial justice.

President Kennedy and civil rights leaders, including Martin Luther King Jr. and John Lewis, meet in the Oval Office in 1963.

Credit: *U.S. News & World Report* magazine collection

CIVIL RIGHTS TIMELINE

1960

John F. Kennedy is elected president.

1961

After white mobs beat Freedom Riders, the Interstate Commerce Commission removes "whites-only" signs from bus terminals, train stations, and airports.

Kennedy Drags His Feet

Kennedy did not want to begin his presidency by fighting for civil rights. The young president was intimidated by older, Southern Democrats. He was convinced these conservative senators would filibuster any law he proposed.

Kennedy hoped to sidestep Congress and rely on his executive power to help Black people. He appointed some African Americans to the executive branch and ordered his cabinet to hire more African Americans in their departments. Kennedy also appointed his brother, Robert F. Kennedy (1928–1965), as U.S. Attorney General and ordered him to follow the letter of the law on civil rights issues.

FILIBUSTER AND CLOTURE

Legislation works its way through Congress on a time schedule. A filibuster is a tactic to run down the clock on a bill by debating nonstop until the time for voting has expired. The only way to stop a filibuster is if two-thirds of senators vote for cloture. Cloture means to end debate and hold a vote on the bill. Do some research on filibusters in history. Why do you think this method was developed? What benefits and drawbacks does it have?

Attorney General Robert F. Kennedy speaking to a crowd of Blacks and whites through a megaphone outside the U.S. Justice Department, 1963

Credit: Warren K. Leffler, *U.S. News & World Report* magazine collection

1963
President Kennedy proposes a civil rights law.

1963
President Kennedy is assassinated by Lee Harvey Oswald in Dallas, Texas, before the civil rights law is passed.

1964
The 1964 Civil Rights law is passed. It bans segregation in public places.

Brothers Robert, Ted, and John Kennedy in 1963

WONDER WHY?

Do today's presidents still see voters in terms of race? Do you think this is how democracy should work?

President Kennedy did not want to get involved in debating the morality of racial equality. He tried to walk a political tightrope, with African Americans on one side and conservative Southern white people on the other. Soon, that tightrope began to shake.

Freedom Rides

Although the U.S. Supreme Court had declared segregated interstate travel unconstitutional, Jim Crow laws remained firmly in place at bus, rail, and airline terminals throughout the South. Separate waiting rooms, restrooms, and restaurants restricted the travel of African Americans.

A sign in a Greyhound bus station in 1943

Freedom Riders are attacked in Alabama, 1961

In the spring of 1961, James Farmer (1920–1999), director of the Congress of Racial Equality (CORE), decided to pressure the federal government to enforce the law with a strategy called the Freedom Rides. Activists planned to ride interstate buses through the Deep South and challenge all segregation they encountered. If white Southerners reacted violently, the federal government would be forced to act. On May 4, 1961, 13 Freedom Riders left Washington, DC, on two buses. The ride went smoothly—until the buses entered Alabama.

> "We were counting on the bigots in the South to do our work for us."
>
> **James Farmer** about the Freedom Rides

Burning Bus

On May 14, one of the buses drove into the terminal at Anniston, Alabama. More than 100 white men surrounded it. They shouted racial slurs, punctured the bus tires, and smashed windows. The driver pulled quickly back onto the highway, but the mob followed.

Minutes later, the Freedom Riders heard the thumping of the bus's flat tires. When the driver pulled in front of a grocery store on the edge of town, the mob swarmed the vehicle. Someone smashed the rear window with a crowbar and tossed in a gas-soaked rag.

Seconds later, the bus was engulfed in flames. When the fuel tank exploded, the mob drew back. Freedom Riders stumbled off the bus, gagging and coughing. They collapsed on the ground, where angry Southerners pummeled them with bats and clubs. Finally, a highway patrol officer fired his pistol in the air and said, "You've had your fun. Let's move back."

WONDER WHY?

Why might public transportation become such a flashpoint of racial tension? Do you think that's the case in your time?

Birmingham

Unaware of what had just happened to their peers, the Freedom Riders on the second bus headed into America's most racist city—Birmingham, Alabama. When this bus pulled into the terminal, a mob of 1,000 people armed with chains, hammers, stakes, and clubs surrounded it. Undaunted, the Freedom Riders got off the bus and entered the white waiting room. The mob attacked.

Several activists were injured. Despite the violence, the Freedom Riders vowed to continue their journey. However, no bus driver would transport them. Traumatized and injured, the activists had ridden as far as they could. They caught a flight out of Birmingham.

A SCENE FROM HELL

Janie Forsyth's (1949–) family owned a store in Anniston, Alabama. On May 14, 1961, the 12-year-old glanced out her living room window and saw a mob of whites gathered around a burning bus in front of the store. Forsyth went outside to find Freedom Riders retching, coughing, and crawling away from the flaming vehicle. "It was like a scene from hell," she recalled. "It was the worst suffering I'd ever heard." Despite the nearby mob, the girl got a bucket of water and went from victim to victim, giving drinks and comforting them.

The Kennedy Brothers' Dilemma

President Kennedy was embarrassed that racial violence in Alabama was making global headlines. Both he and Robert Kennedy were disgusted by the white mob. However, according to Freedom Rider John Lewis (1940–), they were "just as upset with us." The Kennedys thought the activists were asking for trouble.

U.S. Attorney General Robert Kennedy sent his aide, John Seigenthaler (1927–2014), to Alabama to monitor the situation. When Seigenthaler learned the Freedom Riders had boarded a flight out of Birmingham, he went to bed, relieved the crisis was over. But a few hours later, the phone rang.

"Who the hell is Diane Nash," Robert Kennedy demanded.

The FBI had warned Robert Kennedy that a group of college students from Tennessee was headed to Alabama to restart the Freedom Ride. Diane Nash (1938–) was their leader.

John Seigenthaler called Nash and warned that students could be killed. "Sir, you should know," she responded, "we all signed our last will and testaments last night. We cannot let violence overcome nonviolence."

College students had outsmarted the Kennedy brothers.

> "We recognized that if the Freedom Ride was ended right then after all that violence, Southern white racists would think that they could stop a project by inflicting enough violence on it."
>
> **Diane Nash**, leader of Nashville branch of SNCC

DOING WHAT WAS REQUIRED

Having grown up in Chicago, Diane Nash first experienced Jim Crow while at the Tennessee State Fair, where she had to use the "colored only" restrooms. She was frustrated that her Southern Black peers seemed to accept this as a way of life. As leader of the Nashville branch of the Student Nonviolent Coordinating Committee (SNCC), she went to work organizing protests. In 1961, Nash was arrested for training college students in nonviolent resistance. When she refused to move from the whites-only section of the courtroom during her trial, the judge sentenced Nash to 10 days in jail. "I was scared the whole time," she recalled. "But here's the thing—you had to do what was required or you had to tolerate segregation."

Senator James Eastland with President Lyndon B. Johnson in 1968

Bobby Kennedy delivered a message to Alabama Governor John Patterson (1921–). If Patterson would not protect the Freedom Riders, President Kennedy would send federal troops to do the job. Reluctantly, the governor agreed to protect the students.

The next day, state troopers guided the Freedom Riders out of Birmingham while a helicopter guarded them from overhead. When the students' bus reached Montgomery, Alabama, state troopers gave control to Montgomery's public safety commissioner, L.B. Sullivan (1921–1977). Here, things took a turn.

Sullivan had ordered his police officers to stay away from the bus terminal for 30 minutes so the mob could do its work. Armed with baseball bats, pipes, chains, and pitchforks, white men and women attacked the Freedom Riders.

Faced with such defiance, President Kennedy had to act. He sent 400 federal marshals to Montgomery. Then, he publicly asked Alabama officials to "prevent further outbreaks of violence" and urged the Freedom Riders to "refrain from any action . . . to provoke further outbreaks."

A plaque commemorating the Freedom Riders in Birmingham, Alabama

Credit: Kevin from Astoria, NY (CC BY 2.0)

When the bus carrying the Freedom Riders reached Jackson, Mississippi, no mob was waiting. However, state police arrested the activists when they entered the white waiting room. The U.S. Attorney General had made a deal with Mississippi Senator James Eastland (1904–1986). If Mississippi officials guaranteed the safety of the Freedom Riders, President Kennedy would not object if police arrested them for violating Mississippi's segregation laws. The Freedom Riders were sent to the state's maximum security prison. The Kennedys thought that time behind bars would convince the activists to stay off the buses. The Kennedys were wrong.

Supporters from across the country headed to Mississippi. Eventually, 430 people—Black and white—joined the Freedom Rides. Mississippi jails were packed, but people kept coming. The sheer determination of the activists forced the Kennedy administration to change its strategy.

On September 22, 1961, the administration ordered the Interstate Commerce Commission to remove the "whites-only" signs from the nation's bus and train stations and airports. This was an important step forward.

However, the president's actions during the Freedom Rides proved that while Kennedy would preserve order, he would not address civil rights as a moral issue. It took police dogs and fire hoses used against Black children to finally change the president's mind.

WONDER WHY?

What do you know about the Black Lives Matter movement? Are those activists ever arrested?

The Children's March

Birmingham, Alabama, was nicknamed "Bombingham" because, since 1945, there had been more than 50 unsolved bombings in Black neighborhoods. The city was a hotspot of racial tension. Public Safety Commissioner Eugene Connor (1897–1973) and Alabama Governor George Wallace (1919–1998) were both segregationists.

Civil rights leaders came up with a plan to challenge Birmingham's Jim Crow laws. They called the plan Project C—the "C" stood for confrontation. Activists planned to use sit-ins, business boycotts, and mass marches to protest segregation. The campaign was launched on April 4, 1963.

The operation got off to a bad start. On April 12, King and other leaders were arrested. Local white ministers published a joint statement in the newspaper criticizing Project C as "unwise and untimely." They urged local Black people not to participate.

On April 20, the leaders were released from jail, but they knew Project C was in trouble. Not enough locals had volunteered to march—they had jobs and could not afford to be arrested. James Bevel (1936–2008), an activist from Nashville, Tennessee, decided to recruit the city's Black middle school and high school youth, who had no jobs to lose.

On May 2, 1963, 800 students gathered at the 16th Street First Baptist Church to march for equality. Police blocked roads leading away from the church, hoping to contain protestors. But the youth spilled into Kelly Ingram Park, a block that separated the Black district from downtown Birmingham.

> "We were told in some of the mass meetings that the day would come when we could really do something about all of these inequities that we were experiencing."
>
> **Janice Kelsey**, one of the young people who marched

By the end of the day, 500 students were jailed. This alarmed Black adults, and 2,000 people packed the First Baptist Church that evening to prepare for the next morning's march.

WONDER WHY?

What issue do you care enough about to protest? Have you ever been to a demonstration? What was it like?

A statue in Kelly Ingram Park showing Walter Gadsden being attacked by a dog

Credit: Maureen (CC BY 2.0)

The scene horrified the parents who were watching. They hurled bricks and bottles at the firefighters. The peaceful march became a riot, and Commissioner Connor brought out police dogs. Bill Hudson (1932–2010), a photographer with the Associated Press, was in the center of the ruckus. As an officer yanked on the shirt of high school student Walter Gadsden, a police dog lunged for the boy's stomach. Hudson captured the scene with his camera.

But the next day, law enforcement was prepared, too, armed with batons, guns, and high-pressure hoses. As students headed toward Kelly Ingram Park, Commissioner Connor ordered the fire chief to use the hoses on the children. When the chief hesitated, Connor said, "Turn 'em on or go home."

Water exploded from hoses, knocking children to the ground and spinning them across the street. When the youth joined hands to try to stay upright, firefighters funneled two hoses through one nozzle. The force was strong enough to dislodge brick from buildings and tear flesh.

WONDER WHY?

Why do photographs sometimes affect people's perceptions more than words?

JFK Takes a Stand

The next morning, President Kennedy read news articles about the violence in Birmingham. The photograph of the boy facing the snarling police dog deeply disturbed him. By attacking children, segregationists pushed Kennedy to recognize that new federal laws were needed to protect the rights of African Americans. But he wanted to wait for the correct political moment to propose such legislation.

CONNECT

Watch an excerpt of President Kennedy's speech about civil rights at this link. How does he frame civil rights as a moral issue? How were presidential speeches different then from now?

JFK televised civil rights

That moment arrived on June 11, 1963. Alabama Governor George Wallace stood in the door of Tuscaloosa University to block the enrollment of two Black students, and Kennedy had to send federal troops to campus to protect the students and quell the violence. "I may lose the legislation," Kennedy told advisers. "Or I may even lose the election in 1964. But there comes a time when a man has to take a stand."

That evening, in a televised speech, Kennedy addressed the heart of the civil rights struggle. "We are confronted primarily with a moral issue," he told the American people. "It is as old as the scriptures and is as clear as the American Constitution." If the United States was going to hold itself up as a light of freedom around the world, it could not deny freedom to Black people at home. Kennedy asked Congress to pass a law giving all Americans the right to be served at any public facility. No more "whites-only" signs anywhere.

> "Now the time has come for this nation to fulfill its promise."
>
> John F. Kennedy, June 11, 1963

Martin Luther King Jr. was watching the speech in Atlanta, Georgia. When the president proposed the new civil rights law, King leapt to his feet in joy. However, change would not come easily.

The bomb-damaged home of Arthur Shores, NAACP attorney, Birmingham, Alabama, September 1963

Credit: Marion S. Trikosko, *U.S. News & World Report* magazine collection

Kennedy's Legacy

John F. Kennedy did not live to see his civil rights bill become law. On November 22, 1963, the president was assassinated in Dallas, Texas. Vice President Lyndon B. Johnson (1908–1973) was sworn in two hours after Kennedy's death.

On November 27, Johnson addressed Congress, urging lawmakers to honor the slain president by passing his bill. "We have talked long enough in this country about equal rights," Johnson said. "It is time now to write the next chapter . . . in the books of law."

Lyndon B. Johnson taking the oath of office, November 1963

Credit: Cecil W. Stoughton

The bill passed the U.S. House of Representatives on February 10, 1964. But when the legislation reached the U.S. Senate, Southern Democrats began to filibuster. Would the bill die before becoming law?

As the debate droned on, Democratic Senator Hubert Humphrey (1911–1978) and Republican Senate Minority Leader Everett Dirksen (1896–1969) worked behind the scenes. They coaxed, threatened, and begged their colleagues. Finally, after 60 days of nonstop debate, enough senators voted for cloture to end the filibuster. President Johnson signed the Civil Rights Act into law on July 2, 1964.

Word Power!

What vocabulary words did you discover? Can you figure out the meanings of these words? Look in the glossary for help!

activist, assassinate, ban, defiance, discrimination, executive branch, federal, filibuster, justice, provoke, and slur

President Lyndon B. Johnson at the signing the 1964 Civil Rights Act

Credit: O.J. Rapp

Civil Rights Act of 1964

Life for African Americans in the South was transformed after the passing of the Civil Rights Act. Parks, courthouses, restaurants, theaters, sports arenas, and hotels could no longer deny service to Black customers. Employers and labor unions could no longer refuse to hire Black workers. The Equal Employment Opportunity Commission was created to file lawsuits on the behalf of victims of discrimination.

Although the Civil Rights Act of 1964 was a huge step forward, there was still a long way to go. Without political power, African Americans would forever remain second-class citizens. The next battle for civil rights was over the ballot box.

FORGOTTEN HERO—EVERETT DIRKSEN

Republican Senate Minority Leader Everett Dirksen knew the 1964 civil rights bill was too radical to pass the Senate. While hospitalized with a bleeding ulcer, he combed through the legislation and made dozens of changes to create a bill that senators would accept. During the filibuster, Dirksen appealed to the morals of fellow Republicans. On June 10, 1964, he took the Senate floor and spoke. "The time has come for equality of opportunity in sharing in government, in education, and in employment," he said. "It will not be stayed or denied. It is here." Enough Republicans voted to end the filibuster, leading to the passage of the Civil Rights Act.

PROJECT

The Full Picture

Photographs are primary sources that provide a glimpse of a moment in time. However, they are not unbiased. Photographers choose the images they want their audiences to see. Therefore, historians must analyze photographs with care to get the full story.

- **Locate the photograph of teen Walter Gadsden being attacked by a police dog that was printed in newspapers on May 4, 1963.** Examine the foreground and background of the image. What do you think photographer Bill Hudson wanted viewers to see and feel in response to this image?

  Gadsden Times Fowlkes

- **Examine four other photos of Walter Gadsden that Hudson took during the march, available at the Civil Rights Digital Library.** How do these images contradict or support the conclusions you made about the newspaper photo?

  CRDL Walter Gadsden

- **Read the article on this link to learn about what happened to Walter Gadsden on the day of the March.** How does this information change your perspective of what the newspaper photograph shows?

  RTP iconic civil rights

- **Choose one of the unpublished photographs of Gadsden.** Write a newspaper headline and brief story to accompany the image based on your understanding of the incident.

TEXT TO WORLD

What kind of relationship do African Americans have with police officers in your time? Is it different from the Civil Rights Era?

PROJECT

How a Bill Becomes a Law

Investigate the complicated process by which the 1964 Civil Rights Bill became the law of the land. A case history for the bill can be found at the Dirksen Congressional Center.

senate civil rights 1964

- **A helpful resource for the legislative process can be found at *The Kids in the House* website.** Use this information to create a step-by-step flow chart to illustrate how the 1964 Civil Rights Bill became a law.

Kids house 17

- **Correctly use some of the following political terms on your flowchart:**
    - cloture
    - filibuster
    - petition
    - committee
    - mark-up
    - quorum
    - draft
    - constituent
    - veto
    - sponsor

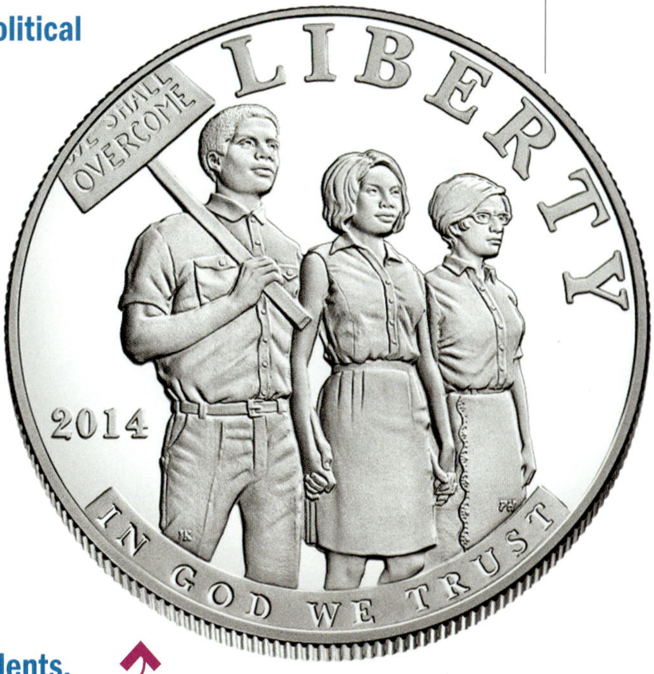

A 2014 commemorative coin honoring the Civil Rights Act of 1964

- **Use the flow chart to teach other students.** How did the proposal President Kennedy made in the summer of 1963 become the law of the land by the summer of 1964?

Civil Rights Movement leader Dr. Ralph David Abernathy and his children walk with Dr. and Mrs. Martin Luther King Jr. on the front line of the march for voting rights.

Credit: The Abernathy family

CHAPTER THREE

WE SHALL OVERCOME

FAST FACTS

WHAT?

The Voting Rights Act of 1965

WHY?

This law outlawed many discriminatory voting practices so African Americans would have a fair shot at voting for whomever they wanted to.

WHEN?

August 6, 1965

HOW?

Protesters peacefully marched to demand voting rights, even as they were subject to a brutal backlash from white Southerners.

The evening of February 18, 1965, Jimmie Lee Jackson (1938–1965) joined several hundred people in Marion, Alabama, on a peaceful voting rights march. He was there because he had tried to register to vote five times in his life—and five times, he had been denied.

Almost as soon as the march began, the protesters were attacked by Alabama state troopers. Jackson took shelter in a nearby cafe with his mother and grandfather, but troopers stormed in. When Jackson came to the aid of his mother, Officer James Fowler shot him twice in the stomach. Eight days later, the 26-year-old died.

African Americans were enraged. James Bevel (1936–2008), an organizer with the Southern Christian Leadership Conference (SCLC), spoke at the young man's memorial service. "We will march Jimmie's body to the state capitol in Montgomery," Bevel said, "and lie it on the steps so Governor George Wallace can see what he's done." Jimmie Lee Jackson had become a martyr in the battle for the right to vote.

CONNECT

Go to the "try to vote" page on this website. What obstacles did officials erect to prevent African Americans from voting?

PLEASE BE AWARE THAT THERE IS SOME DISTURBING IMAGERY ON THIS WEBSITE.

Thirteen Jim Crow voting

Voter Suppression during Jim Crow

The Fifteenth Amendment granted Black men the right to vote in 1870, and the Nineteenth Amendment did the same for Black women in 1920. But reality was quite different from the ideal. Southern states simply built other barriers to block African Americans from exercising their right to vote.

Economic pressure was a powerful roadblock. Southern states required voters to pay a poll tax before they could vote—and for many, this was an impossible expense. Even African Americans who could afford the tax faced other financial barriers. Banks denied them loans. Landlords threatened to evict them. Employers fired them. Many African Americans simply stopped voting.

Literacy tests were another obstacle. Some states required voters to interpret a section of a state's constitution. The county clerk, always a white man, determined whether the person passed the test or not. The clerks chose simple sentences for whites and complicated passages whenever they wanted someone to fail.

CIVIL RIGHTS TIMELINE

1865
The Ku Klux Klan is founded.

January 2, 1965
Martin Luther King Jr. launches a massive voting rights campaign.

February 18, 1965
Police kill Jimmie Lee Jackson while he is marching peacefully for voting rights.

HOW MANY SEEDS IN THE WATERMELON?

In 1960, when Georgia resident Clarence Gaskins, who was an African American, went to vote, the official showed him a jar of corn, a bar of soap, a watermelon, and a cucumber. In order to vote, he had to correctly guess how many kernels were in the jar, how many bubbles were in the soap, how many seeds were in the watermelon, and how many bumps were on the cucumber. This was one of many ways African Americans were denied the right to vote. Gaskins left without trying—he knew the system was against him.

States also passed grandfather clauses. This rule allowed people to avoid paying a poll tax or passing a literacy test if their grandfather had been qualified to vote before the Civil War. Who would have been voting in the South before the Civil War? Certainly not African Americans, most of whom would have been slaves.

CONNECT

Read an article about the first Black man to vote in the United States, Thomas Mundy Peterson.

first Black voter

Violence was an ever-present threat to any African American determined to vote. The Ku Klux Klan rode out at night to terrorize Black families. African Americans risked destruction of property, rape, and lynching if they dared vote.

The *Harper's Weekly* cartoon shows criticism of the literacy tests given to African Americans before they could vote. What point is the cartoonist trying to make?

Credit: *Harper's Weekly*, 1879

March 7, 1965
On "Bloody Sunday," Alabama state police use force to prevent civil rights marchers from crossing the Edmund Pettis Bridge.

March 15, 1965
President Johnson announces that he is sending a voting rights bill to Congress.

March 25, 1965
Civil rights activists arrive in Montgomery, Alabama, after successfully completing their march from Selma.

August 6, 1965
President Johnson signs the Voting Rights Bill into law.

The Ku Klux Klan in Virginia, 1922

Voter suppression methods were effective. In 1896, there were 130,334 African Americans registered to vote in Louisiana. By 1904, that number had plunged to 1,342. Not a single Black person voted in the 1904 presidential election in Virginia or South Carolina.

This pattern continued through the decades. In 1965, the population of Selma, Alabama, was more than 50 percent Black. However, only 383 of the 15,000 African Americans living in the city were registered to vote.

Jurors are drawn from lists of registered voters—anyone not registered is excluded from juries. Black people accused of crimes were judged by all-white juries, often with terrible results. In 1958, a Black man named James Wilson was convicted of stealing $1.95 from his employer. An all-white jury sentenced him to death and the all-white Alabama Supreme Court upheld the sentence. Does this seem fair?

WONDER WHY?

Why were Southern whites so threatened by the idea of African Americans voting? What might their vote have changed? Do you see this dynamic in today's politics?

Although almost 2,000 African American men had been elected to political office during Reconstruction, the period after the Civil War between 1863 and 1877, this participation all but vanished during the Jim Crow era. In 1965, there were no Black members of the U.S. Senate, no Black governors, and only six African American members of the House.

CONNECT

Read an 1868 warning the Klan gave to Davie Jeems, a Black man elected sheriff in Lincoln County, Georgia. How would this notice affect a Black person's desire to vote?

PLEASE BE AWARE THIS LETTER CONTAINS SENSITIVE LANGUAGE.

Gilderlehrman 09090p1

Voting Rights Campaign

In his January 1965 State of the Union address, President Lyndon B. Johnson said he intended to get rid of "every remaining obstacle to the right and opportunity to vote." However, the president had other priorities first.

Johnson's Great Society was a collection of social programs designed to help the poor. To pass these programs, he needed support from Southern congressmen. Therefore, he wanted to wait before proposing a voting rights law.

First African American senator and representatives in the 41st and 42nd Congress of the United States, 1872: Senator Hiram Revels of Mississippi and Representatives Benjamin Turner of Alabama, Robert De Large of South Carolina, Josiah Walls of Florida, Jefferson Long of Georgia, and Joseph Rainey and Robert B. Elliot of South Carolina

Selma, Alabama
Credit: Peter Pettus

Civil rights leaders had no intention of waiting for Johnson to take the lead. In Selma, Alabama, on January 2, 1965, Martin Luther King Jr. announced a massive campaign to register Black Alabamians to vote. He expected officials to use force to stop them. "We must be ready to march," King warned. "We must be ready to go to jail by the thousands." The hope was that media attention would pressure Congress to pass a law to enforce Black voting rights.

STATS ON SELMA

Despite the 1954 *Brown* decision and the 1964 Civil Rights Act, Selma remained segregated. Schools, restaurants, drinking fountains, and public bathrooms were divided by race. Selma was the county seat of Dallas County, a county with 15,115 Black citizens of voting age. However, in 1965 only 156 of those residents were registered to vote. Today, voter ID laws and limited polling places in Black neighborhoods aid in voter suppression.

"Jimmie Lee Jackson is speaking to us from the casket, and he is saying that we must substitute courage for caution."
Martin Luther King Jr., 1965

With a pistol on one hip and a cattle prod on the other, Sheriff Jim Clark (1922–2007) was the Jim Crow enforcer in Dallas County, Alabama. He was aided by Circuit Court Judge James Hare (1906–1969), who banned activists from gathering in groups of more than three people.

On January 18, local African Americans marched in large groups to the Selma courthouse to register to vote. Sheriff Clark arrested them. However, they posted bail and returned on the next registration day. So, Clark ordered his officers to remove protestors by force if necessary. They started by arresting Martin Luther King Jr. on February 1.

President Johnson was monitoring the situation. To calm tensions, Johnson announced plans to send a voting rights bill to Congress by the end of the year. But then, Jimmie Lee Jackson was murdered. The time had come to march.

WONDER WHY?

What is the more effective method of expressing your feelings about a social problem—protest marches or comments on social media? Why might this be the case?

"Bloody Sunday"

The protesters' plan was to march 54 miles from Selma to the state capital in Montgomery, Alabama. At the end of the journey, protestors would petition state officials to grant Black voting rights. However, the evening before the march, Governor Wallace declared it an unauthorized assembly. He ordered state police to prevent activists from leaving Selma.

> "I thought I was going to die."
>
> **John Lewis** recalling the "Bloody Sunday" march in 1965

On March 7, state police commander Albert Lingo (1910–1969) assembled officers on the far side of the Edmund Pettis Bridge, which led across the Alabama River east of Selma. At least 300 marchers crossed the bridge and came face to face with state troopers. When ordered to leave, the protestors stood their ground.

The troopers, including some on horseback, charged into the demonstrators, trampling people who fell. Officers fired tear gas into the crowd. As the marchers ran, police swung their batons into skulls and limbs. White spectators lining the road cheered. A total of 56 marchers were injured.

People on the Civil Rights March in Selma, Alabama

Credit: Peter Pettus

The following day, photographs of "Bloody Sunday" made the front page. Martin Luther King Jr. announced that marchers would try again in a few days. Volunteers from across the country headed to Selma to join the demonstration.

Johnson Takes a Stand

President Johnson knew he had to act. Instead of sending in federal troops as previous presidents had, he chose a different strategy. On the evening of March 15, Johnson gave a televised address before a packed chamber in the U.S. House of Representatives.

Johnson dove into the heart of the issue. "I speak tonight for the dignity of man and the destiny of democracy." He said Bloody Sunday was a turning point in the nation's quest for freedom. Johnson's voice rose as he insisted that even if the United States could "defeat every enemy, . . . double our wealth, and conquer the stars," if it could not grant equality to its citizens, "then we will have failed as a people and as a nation."

The applause was thunderous. For the first time in American history, a president had identified the values of the nation with the cause of racial equality.

Then, Johnson laid out his plan for a national voting rights law. He called on Congress to pass a law to enforce Black voting rights in areas where local officials had long denied them this right. At the close of the speech, President Johnson slowly and deliberately spoke the phrase civil rights workers had been using for years. "We—shall—overcome." With that word "we," Johnson was standing side-by-side with the Civil Rights Movement. The audience rose to its feet, and the applause lasted a long time.

WONDER WHY?

How has public perception about police violence against African Americans changed since the Civil Rights Movement?

CONNECT

Listen to parts of Johnson's March 15 speech. Can you think of any recent political speeches that drew this much applause?

Johnson speech March 15

Activists march in New York City in solidarity with people in Alabama, 1965.

Credit: Stanley Wolfson, *New York World Telegram & Sun*

Voting Rights Act of 1965

Support for the Civil Rights Movement surged throughout the nation. A Gallup poll in the spring of 1965 showed that four out of five Americans favored a voting rights law.

The legislation President Johnson sent to Congress prohibited all practices that denied someone the right to vote on the basis of race or color. This included literacy tests and poll taxes. Communities where less than 50 percent of nonwhite voters were registered to vote were placed under federal oversight. They could not change their voting rules without permission from the U.S. Attorney General or a federal judge.

> "Because it is not just Negroes, but really it is all of us, who must overcome the crippling legacy of bigotry and injustice."
>
> **President Johnson, 1965**

As expected, when the bill came up for debate in the Senate on April 22, Southern lawmakers filibustered. Supporters of the bill worked behind the scenes, calling in favors and making deals. On May 25, the Senate voted for cloture, killing the filibuster. On May 26, the Senate passed the voting rights bill on a vote of 77 to 19. The bill overwhelmingly passed the House on August 3. Three days later, President Johnson signed it into law.

Demonstrators outside the White House, 1965

Credit: Warren K. Leffler, *U.S. News & World Report* magazine collection

SUCCESSFUL MARCH

On March 21, 1965, 1,400 civil rights protestors set out on foot from Selma. This time, no state troopers blocked their way. When the marchers reached the outskirts of Montgomery a few days later, their ranks had swelled to 1,200. Martin Luther King Jr. addressed 25,000 supporters from the steps of the state capitol while Governor Wallace watched from behind the blinds of his office window.

What Happened Afterward

It took time for African Americans to overcome their fear and discouragement after decades of being denied the right to vote. It wasn't as simple as flipping a switch. Throughout the remainder of his presidency, Johnson badgered activists to launch voter registration drives. "I don't care if you are Mexican, American, Negro, Baptist, Catholic, Jew—just vote," Johnson told NAACP director Roy Wilkins. The president was convinced that if people voted, democracy and justice would follow.

The 50th anniversary of Bloody Sunday, 2015

By the summer of 1965, federal agencies had identified counties in Alabama, Mississippi, Louisiana, and Georgia where less than 50 percent of the Black voting age population was registered. Officials got to work. By the end of January 1966, almost 94,000 new voters were registered, most of them African Americans. By the 1968 presidential election, 62 percent of eligible southern Black people were registered to vote.

Voting rights alone could not guarantee racial equality. African Americans in Northern states had been voting for decades, yet many of them lived in slums with high unemployment and crime rates. It was clear more progress was needed.

Next, the battle for civil rights headed to Northern cities.

Word Power!

What vocabulary words did you discover? Can you figure out the meanings of these words? Look in the glossary for help!

bigotry, equality, exclude, injustice, interpret, legacy, literacy, poll tax, Reconstruction, and suppression

DON'T THROW AWAY THE UMBRELLA

In 2013, the U.S. Supreme Court changed a key provision of the Voting Rights Act. Section Five prevented local officials in counties with a history of racial discrimination from making changes to their elections processes without permission from the federal government. But in the *Shelby County v. Holder* case, the U.S. Supreme Court ruled in a 5-4 decision that this clause was no longer necessary. Justice Ruth Bader Ginsberg (1933–) dissented. She wrote that it was ridiculous to throw out a rule that was working. She compared it to "throwing away your umbrella in a rainstorm because you are not getting wet."

PROJECT

Voter Suppression 2.0

Many states have passed laws that make it harder for people to vote. These include ending same-day voter registration, ending "motor voter" registration, imposing residency requirements that affect college students, passing voter ID laws, restricting voting for people with felony convictions, and purging voter lists.

President Lyndon B. Johnson meets with Martin Luther King Jr. at the signing of the Voting Rights Act of 1965.

Credit: Yoichi Okamoto

- **Research one of the restrictions listed above that make it harder to vote.**
- **Design a poster or pamphlet to inform the public about how this restriction affects the right to vote.** To what extent does it affect people of color more than white people?

CONNECT

Go to this link to play the "Voter Suppression Trail." How do a person's race, ethnicity, and location affect their ability to vote? What explains these differences?

everyday arcade voter

TEXT TO WORLD

Do you know anyone who's had difficulty voting? What happened? How could the situation have been prevented?

PROJECT

Packing and Cracking

In a democracy, everyone's vote is supposed to count. However, in most states, the political party in control of the state government redraws congressional and state legislative district boundaries every 10 years. These boundaries determine who votes in each district. Politicians usually draw boundary lines to give their party an advantage. This is called political gerrymandering and it is usually legal. Racial gerrymandering, when politicians redraw legislative district lines to reduce the political power of racial minorities, is illegal under the 1965 Voting Rights Act. However, political gerrymandering has a racial impact.

- **Prepare to redraw legislative districts in the fictitious state of Gerryland.** This will help you to evaluate the impact of political gerrymandering.

- **Below is Gerryland.** Based on its population, the state should get three congressional districts. Because two-thirds of voters support the Blue Party, political leaders from this party get to draw congressional district lines.

Watch the video *Gerrymandering: Is Geometry Silencing Your Vote*? and define the terms "cracking" and "packing."

above the noise gerrymandering

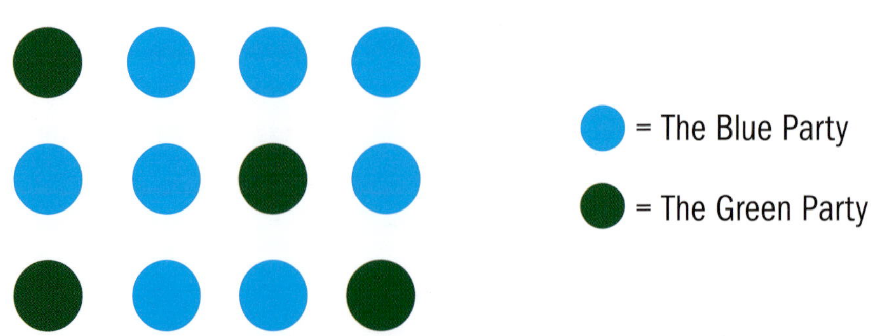

PROJECT

- **Imagine you belong to the Blue Party.** Draw lines to create three districts. Each district must have the same number of voters. Draw the lines in order to give the Blue Party total control of the state.

- **As years pass, some Blue Party supporters move out of Gerryland and more Green Party supporters move in.** Although the population size remains the same, voters are split evenly between the Green Party and the Blue Party. Redraw district lines to "crack" up Green Party supporters into different districts to weaken their power.

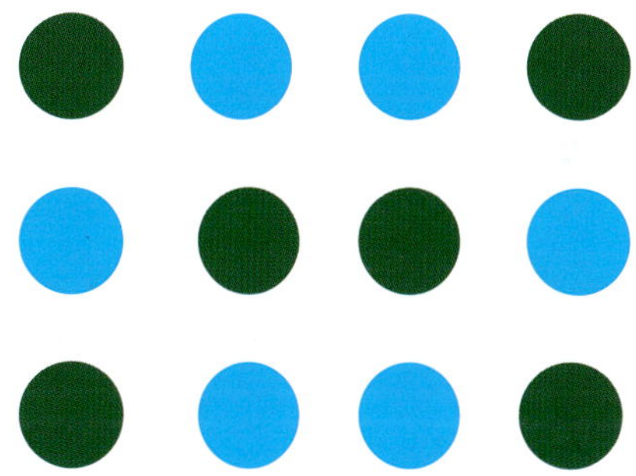

- **Ten years later, the population of Gerryland has grown.** Add three new voters to indicate this. Now, three-fifths of Gerryland voters support the Green Party. But as a Blue Party politician, you want to maintain your control over the government. Redraw district lines to pack as many Green Party supporters as possible into one district.

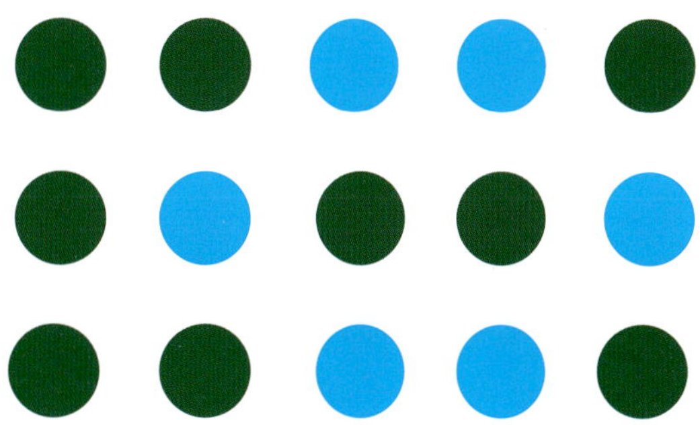

- **Consider the consequences.** How would you feel if you were a voter who belonged to the Green Party? How might political gerrymandering have a negative impact on nonwhite voters, even though racial gerrymandering is illegal? How can you redraw district lines to create a fair division based on population and political party support? What are some possible solutions to the problems caused by political gerrymandering?

A sign at the Sojourner Truth homes in Detroit, Michigan, 1942

Credit: Arthur Siegel

CHAPTER FOUR

DOORS OF OPPORTUNITY

On August 11, 1965, a white police officer pulled over a man in the poor Black neighborhood of Watts in Los Angeles, California. A crowd gathered as the officer pushed the man into the patrol car. Onlookers began to pelt the officer with bottles and rocks. Police called for reinforcements and the violence escalated. Angry African Americans looted stores, attacked white people, and firebombed businesses.

FAST FACTS

WHAT?

The Fair Housing Act

WHY?

This law banned discrimination in the sale, rental, or financing of housing.

WHEN?

April 11, 1968

HOW?

As riots erupted across the United States in reaction to unfair treatment in terms of housing, politicians worked to pass a bill that would equalize everyone's opportunities to pursue housing.

When President Johnson learned of the rioting, he felt despair. "How is it possible," he asked, "after all we've accomplished." For six days, Watts was a war zone. When things finally settled, 34 people were dead, 1,000 injured, and 4,000 arrested, and the neighborhood lay in smoldering ruins.

The Watts riot was only a prelude. The following summer, Black youth rioted in 38 cities.

The Civil Rights Movement had addressed the evils of segregation, but had not touched high unemployment, poor schools, decaying housing, and police brutality—problems that plagued African Americans living in inner cities.

CONNECT

Watch news footage of the Watts riot. What kind of language does the newscaster use to make it sound like the fault of African Americans?

Watts Riot AP

A tenant farmer's home in Arkansas, 1935

Credit: Ben Shahn

CIVIL RIGHTS TIMELINE

August 1965–August 1966
The Chicago Freedom Movement tries to desegregate Chicago's housing.

August 11–16, 1965
Riots destroy the Black neighborhood of Watts in Los Angeles, California.

Institutional Racism Created Urban Slums

America's cities divided along racial lines more than a century ago. As African Americans began migrating north in the early twentieth century, government policies excluded them from white communities.

Crowded living quarters in Chicago, Illinois, 1941

Credit: Farm Security Administration

During the Great Depression of the 1930s, unemployment was high and wages were low. Homeowners struggled to make their mortgage payments. To stabilize the shaky housing market, the federal government created the Home Owners Loan Corp (HOLC) and the Federal Housing Administration (FHA). These agencies refinanced loans to lower mortgage payments and insured loans to protect bankers willing to lend people money.

CONNECT

For decades, "sundown towns" existed across the United States. African Americans were banned from living in or even staying overnight in these communities. Go to this link to find the possible sundown towns in your state.

sundown towns search

March 1968
The Kerner Commission concludes that white racism causes the urban violence that plagues American cities.

April 4, 1968
Martin Luther King Jr. is assassinated in Memphis, Tennessee.

April 11, 1968
President Johnson signs the Civil Rights Act of 1968, outlawing discrimination in housing.

FHA housing in San Diego, California, 1941

Credit: Russell Lee

However, both the HOLC and the FHA considered African American homebuyers a risky investment, so they began a practice called "redlining." Officials created color-coded maps of neighborhoods, shading areas with large Black populations in red. The federal government refused to grant loans to people who lived in redlined areas.

After World War II ended in 1945, American soldiers returned home, got married, and their families began to grow. The country did not have enough affordable housing to meet the needs of this baby boom. Therefore, in 1949, Congress passed the Housing Act. This law authorized the government to build 800,000 low-rent housing units. But the projects were segregated, and most units were reserved for whites.

By the 1950s, the economy was booming and the middle class swelled. Construction companies received low-interest loans from the FHA to build houses on the edges of cities. The suburbs were born. Mass-produced, three-bedroom houses cost less than $8,000. This is the equivalent of about $76,535 today.

Young boys harassing the Horace Baker family, the first African American family to move into the all-white Delmar Village neighborhood of Folcroft, Pennsylvania, 1963

But when African Americans made offers on these houses, their applications were rejected. Between 1934 and 1968, 98 percent of the loans approved by the federal government went to whites. Those few African Americans who managed to buy a home in an all-white community faced harassment and violence.

CONNECT

Watch a video on how white neighbors treated the Horace Baker family, the first Black family to move into an all-white suburb in Folcroft, Pennsylvania, in 1963. What were the reasons whites gave for not wanting Blacks living in their community?

LOC white backlash

Without access to loans, African Americans were trapped in urban neighborhoods while whites fled to the suburbs. As more African Americans migrated from the South, demand for housing in the cities outpaced supply. Prices soared. Black people paid more to rent second-rate houses in the city than it would have cost them to buy new, suburban homes.

WONDER WHY?

What benefits come from living in a neighborhood with people from different racial, ethnic, religious, and national backgrounds?

In 1965, Martin Luther King Jr.'s family paid $94 a month for a broken-down, four-bedroom apartment in Chicago, while a new, five-bedroom apartment in a nearby white subdivision cost only $78 a month.

THE COSTS OF REDLINING

The wealth owned by middle-class families comes in part from the value of their houses. By the time the law changed to permit African Americans to buy homes in all-white communities, these houses were more than most people could afford. Homes that cost $8,000 in 1950 sell for between $300,000 and $400,000 today. Because African Americans were prevented from purchasing affordable homes decades ago, their personal wealth has been stunted. In 2016, the average white family owned 10 times more wealth than the average Black family. What other historical patterns can you see affecting wealth today?

Life in the Inner City

While urban Black communities had rich cultures full of music, literature, and art, individuals lived in stark poverty. Rats and roaches overran crowded tenements. Broken stairs and peeling walls were never repaired. Corrupt deals and rigged elections kept political power in the hands of those leaders who failed to enforce health and safety laws and hold slum landlords accountable.

A sign for FHA housing in San Diego, California, 1941

Credit: Russell Lee

Seattle, Washington, U.S. fair housing protest, 1964

Credit: Courtesy of the Seattle Municipal Archives

Segregation affected more than the buildings African Americans lived in. White employers moved to the suburbs, taking the best jobs with them. Public transportation rarely ran to the suburbs, so if a Black person could not afford a car, those good-paying jobs would be out of reach.

THE POLITICS OF RATS

In 1967, President Johnson proposed the Rat Extermination Act to fund the killing of millions of rats that bred in inner cities. The bill was expected to pass Congress easily. But after African Americans rioted in Newark, New Jersey, in July, southern Democrats and Republican congressmen blocked the bill. Lawmakers suggested Johnson hire an army of cats instead. The president was furious. He reminded lawmakers that federal money was used to protect cows from rodents and said, "The least we can do is give our children the same protection we give our livestock." Congress eventually passed the law.

Because people lived in segregated neighborhoods, schools were naturally segregated. Wealthy suburban schools prepared white students for college and careers, while city schools were overcrowded and understaffed. Children slipped through the cracks. For example, in the 1960s, two-thirds of teens in the Black and Latino neighborhood of Harlem, New York, did not graduate from high school. Civil rights activists vowed to force the federal government to change this grim reality.

CONNECT

How integrated is your city? Go to the map at this website. In the box below the map, type the name of your city. What is the largest racial group in your community? What factors might explain the diversity or lack of diversity in your community? Why does this matter?

Washington Post **segregation cities**

The Chicago Freedom Movement

Chicago, Illinois, was one of the most segregated cities in the country. In July 1965, leaders of the Chicago Council of Community Organizations (CCCO) invited Martin Luther King Jr. and the Southern Christian Leadership Conference (SCLC) to help them fight for open housing.

> "The land of rats and roaches where a nickel costs a dime."
>
> Langston Hughes (1902–1967), writer, on inner-city living

This would allow African Americans to buy homes in any area they could afford.

Chicago's political scene was tightly controlled by Mayor Richard Daley (1902–1976). Because he had supported African Americans running for office in Chicago, King thought Chicago was the right city to launch an open housing campaign. Bayard Rustin (1912–1987), one of King's advisers, disagreed. Rustin warned King, "You don't know what Chicago is like . . . there are powerful political figures . . . . You're going to be wiped out."

WONDER WHY?

How does the neighborhood you live in impact your future? Do you think things have changed since the 1960s?

Bayard Rustin in 1964

Credit: *New York World-Telegram and the Sun* staff photographer

King went ahead despite Rustin's concerns. In the spring of 1966, the CCOO and SCLC organized local African Americans. When summer arrived, they began to march through white neighborhoods, demanding the right to live where they chose.

Mayor Daley was a shrewd politician. He had no intention of making the mistakes Southern officials had made when faced with civil rights protests. Daley granted the activists permission to march and ordered police to form a buffer between the marchers and white citizens.

Violence erupted anyway.

In one white neighborhood on August 5, a mob of hundreds threw bottles, bricks, and rocks at marchers. One rock hit King in the head, bringing him to his knees. As the summer continued, the size and anger of the mobs grew.

Support for the Civil Rights Movement fell that summer. White Americans viewed the Black people marching for open housing and the Black people rioting in inner cities as one and the same.

By the end of August, King and Daley were ready to negotiate. The result was the Summit Agreement. Chicago officials agreed to enforce an open housing law that had been passed three years earlier but ignored. The Chicago Real Estate Board promised to urge its members to rent and sell homes to African Americans in white neighborhoods. In return, the activists would stop marching.

However, there was no way to guarantee when or even if Chicago officials would keep their promises. Though King declared the agreement a "victory for justice," most activists believed the Chicago Freedom Movement had failed.

> "I think on the whole, I've never seen as much hate and hostility."
>
> **Martin Luther King Jr.** about hostility in Chicago's white neighborhoods

Factors That Forced Change

Riots broke out in more than 100 cities during the summer of 1967. Some conservatives blamed President Johnson's Great Society programs for giving too much government aid to poor Black communities. Others blamed civil rights activists for stirring things up. Whites demanded a return to law and order.

President Johnson appointed a panel of experts called the Kerner Commission to investigate the causes of the urban violence and propose solutions. In March 1968, the commission released a conclusion that shocked many white Americans. The report stated, "White society is deeply implicated in the ghetto. White institutions created it, white institutions maintain it, and white society condones it." It was hard to ignore the charge: Urban violence was caused by white racism.

AMERICA ON FIRE

Social protests turned into riots across the United States in the spring of 2020. The focus of the media often became the looting and property damage instead of the ongoing violence against African Americans that people were originally protesting against. King once said, "A riot is the language of the unheard." How does this apply to protesters?

> "Our nation is moving toward two societies, one Black, one white—separate and unequal."
> The Kerner Commission

The Kerner Commission's conclusion pushed President Johnson to work harder for an open housing law. For two years, he had tried and failed to get one through Congress. In 1966, Johnson posed a civil rights law that would have banned discrimination in the sale and rental of housing, but the Senate filibustered it to death.

The following year, Johnson tried again. On February 15, 1967, he delivered a special message to Congress. He said, "I am proposing fair housing legislation again this year because it is decent and right." But again, conservative senators killed the bill.

Johnson refused to give up. The bill came up for debate again in 1968, and once more conservative senators began to filibuster. This time, the president worked on Senator Dirksen's conscience.

WONDER WHY?

During the urban riots of the 1960s, African Americans looted businesses and burned buildings in their own neighborhoods. This happened again in 2020. What explains this self-destructive behavior?

President Lyndon B. Johnson with some members of the National Advisory Commission on Civil Disorders (the Kerner Commission) in the Cabinet Room of the White House, Washington, DC, 1967

Dirksen did not support open housing and had refused to support the bill previously. However, he was as alarmed about the urban rioting as Johnson. Dirksen convinced Johnson to exclude owner-occupied residences with fewer than four units from the law, and the two men made a deal.

"In order for us as poor and oppressed people to become a part of a society that is meaningful, the system under which we now exist has to be radically changed."

Ella Baker (1903–1986), civil rights leader

For the third time during Johnson's president, the Senate voted for cloture. On March 4, 1968, the filibuster ended and the Senate passed the Civil Rights Act of 1968. But the House of Representatives still needed to approve it.

House conservatives hated the bill, and debate dragged on endlessly. When the House adjourned the afternoon of April 4, 1968, the bill seemed certain to fail. Then tragedy struck, giving President Johnson an opportunity.

The Aftermath of Assassination

The evening of April 4, 1968, Martin Luther King Jr. stepped out on the balcony of his hotel room in Memphis, Tennessee. From a boarding house across the street, assassin James Earl Ray (1928–1998) fired a single bullet that struck King in the face.

As word of King's murder got out, riots rocked the nation. In Washington, DC, more than 700 fires turned nighttime into day. President Johnson had to act fast.

VIOLENCE AFTER KING'S DEATH

For 10 days after King's death, grieving and angry African Americans rioted in 125 cities. In the greatest domestic uprising since the Civil War, 3,500 people were injured, 43 killed, and 27,000 arrested. President Johnson ordered 4,000 soldiers to cordon off the White House, and 70,000 Army and National Guard members were deployed in 29 states.

CONNECT

View images of some of the riots that erupted after King's death. Why do you think the commentators are all people in law enforcement? What might someone who was rioting say differently about the experience?

everything was on fire YouTube

Workers listen to news of King's death.
Credit: Kheel Center, Cornell University (CC BY 2.0)

Johnson begged Congress to "guarantee a basic American right—the right of a man to secure a home for his family regardless of the color of his skin." As the nation's capital burned and rioting ruptured cities across the country, 21 Republican representatives crossed party lines to support the housing law. On April 10, 1968, the House passed the Civil Rights Act of 1968. President Johnson signed it into law the next day.

"We have passed many civil rights pieces of legislation. But none is more important than this."
President Johnson, 1968

The Fair Housing Law's Strengths and Weaknesses

The 1968 Civil Rights Law has been somewhat effective at reducing individual acts of housing discrimination, but it has not succeeded in integrating neighborhoods.

For the first time in history, the law made it illegal for people to refuse to rent or sell to someone based on their race. Realtors could no longer steer homebuyers to certain neighborhoods based on skin color. The law created a civil rights division within the U.S. Department of Housing and Urban Development (HUD) to investigate complaints of housing discrimination. If a developer was found guilty, HUD could deny them federal funding.

But many white Americans were determined to keep their neighborhoods segregated. These attitudes would not change unless the law was strictly enforced—and the Fair Housing Act had weak enforcement mechanisms.

Word Power!

What vocabulary words did you discover? Can you figure out the meanings of these words? Look in the glossary for help!

brutality, diversity, ethnic, institutional racism, migrate, open housing, riot, slum, sundown town, and tenement

Soldiers stand guard near the U.S. Capitol during the 1968 riots

Credit: Warren K. Leffler *U.S. News & World Report* magazine collection

The law required victims of discrimination to file a formal complaint with HUD or sue in federal court. This was expensive and time-consuming. Even if HUD found a property owner guilty of discrimination, the agency could not punish the owner. The agency could only refer cases to the attorney general. But the attorney general could only prosecute if the property owner showed a pattern of discrimination.

So, although housing discrimination declined after 1968, it did not disappear. According to the National Fair Housing Alliance, there were 28,181 complaints of housing discrimination in 2016.

Statistics prove that, even in the twenty-first century, Americans live in segregated neighborhoods. According to the National Fair Housing Alliance, 50 percent of African Americans and 40 percent of Latinos lived in neighborhoods with no white people in 2020, and whites lived in communities where 80 percent of residents were also white. While some of this is due to housing discrimination, most is a result of income inequality. Whites can afford to buy homes in more expensive neighborhoods than most people of color can.

Following the assassination of Martin Luther King Jr. and the passage of the Fair Housing Law, the Civil Rights Movement reached a turning point. A generational divide opened between leaders. While older activists still believed nonviolent resistance was the key to improving life for African Americans, young leaders took a confrontational approach. As a result, white Americans responded with a backlash at the ballot box. We'll see how this played out in the next chapter.

Johnson signing the Civil Rights Bill, April 11, 1968

Credit: Warren K. Leffler, *U.S. News & World Report* magazine collection

PROJECT

Unifying Graffiti

During the 1940s in Detroit, Michigan, developers built a half-mile long, six-foot-high concrete wall to separate their all-white community from the nearby black neighborhood. The wall still stands as a symbol of the racist policies of the past. But today, a mural with symbols of unity and progress cover the wall.

- **Work with peers to design a mural to reflect history, values, and beliefs that unite your community.** Decide on the message you want to communicate about what is good and strong about your community.
- **Sketch images on a large piece of banner paper.**
- **Paint the final version of the mural.** Display it in a public space.

A protest mural in Minneapolis, Minnesota, 2020

TEXT TO WORLD

How has where you live affected where you go to school? Where your family works? Whether or not you'll go to college?

PROJECT

Rigged Monopoly

The board game *Monopoly* was invented in the early 1900s to simulate the business world. Rewrite *Monopoly*'s rules to reflect how race-based housing policies create economic injustices for a certain group of people.

- **First, define the following vocabulary:** assets, liabilities, wealth gap, mortgage, redlining.
- **Play the game with friends or classmates following the original rules.** As you play, keep a record of the following:
  - Each player's income (how much money you have on hand per turn)
  - Accumulated wealth (how much money you have when the game stops)
  - A list of property each player owns at the end of the game
- **Decide who will represent Green players and who will represent Orange players.** Rewrite the rules to reflect the realities of life before the Fair Housing Law was passed. Create challenges, such as redlining, violence and intimidation, and lack of public transportation. Use Post-it notes to change the wording on the game board and on Community Chest and Chance cards.
- **Play the revised version of the game, again keeping an accounting of each player's income, wealth, and property.** Play once with Green as disadvantaged and once with Orange as disadvantaged.
  - How do the two versions of the game compare?
  - How do you feel playing the second version?

CONNECT

Can someone who has never experienced or witnessed racism learn about it? During the 1960s, a teacher named Jane Elliot developed a method to do this based on eye color. Read an article and watch a video about her teachings at this website.

People Jane Elliot

The 1967 Pulitzer Prize-winning photo of James Meredith after being shot during a march in 1966

Credit: Jack R. Thornell, Associated Press

CHAPTER FIVE

BLACK POWER

FAST FACTS

WHAT?
A Black Power movement that encouraged racial pride, self-sufficiency, and equality.

WHY?
Despite the gains made through laws that addressed integrated schools and equal housing, Black people were still at a disadvantage when it came to wealth and financial independence.

WHEN?
Mid 1960s

HOW?
When more funding was invested in Black businesses and institutions, African Americans were able to earn more and find a level of self-sufficiency that had previously been out of reach.

On June 7, 1966, James Meredith (1933–) set out from Memphis, Tennessee, on a "March Against Fear." He planned to walk all the way to Jackson, Mississippi, to "challenge the . . . overriding fear" African Americans felt when they tried to register to vote.

Meredith did not get far. On the second day of the march, someone shot him. Refusing to give in to terror, other activists picked up where Meredith left off.

On June 16, the marchers reached Greenwood, Mississippi, and set up tents around a Black elementary school. Police ordered them to leave, but 24-year-old Stokely Carmichael (1941–1998), the new chairman of SNCC, refused. Police arrested him.

After being released on bond, Carmichael addressed a crowd with fiery words. "This is the 27th time I have been arrested—and I ain't going to jail no more . . . . The only way we gonna stop them white men from whuppin' us is to take over. We been saying freedom for six years and we ain't got nothin'. What we gonna start saying now is Black Power!"

The emergence of Black Power as a slogan created a firestorm both within the Civil Rights Movement and the larger society.

An Asian American man showing support of Black Power, 1968

Credit: Howard L. Bingham

CIVIL RIGHTS TIMELINE

June 6–25, 1966
In the March Against Fear, activists walk from Memphis, Tennessee, to Jackson, Mississippi.

October 15, 1966
The Black Panther Party is founded.

May 27, 1968
In *Green v. School Board of New Kent County*, the U.S. Supreme Court creates guidelines to determine when a school district is desegregated.

Black Power

At its core, Black Power was a belief in racial pride, self-sufficiency, and equality. Beyond that, the slogan meant different things to different people. Some African Americans believed if they united to form their own political, economic, and social institutions, they could live peacefully with whites. Others feared Black people would always be oppressed, so they wanted complete separation—a separate black nation-state.

Black Power split the Civil Rights Movement in two. Leaders of SNCC and CORE decided allying with white liberals had not helped them achieve equality, so they expelled their white members. They also abandoned the strategy of nonviolence, insisting Blacks had the right to self-defense.

WONDER WHY?

Which party do you think was right, the group that thought violence was part of the answer or the one that thought any kind of violence was wrong? Why?

"Integration . . . has been based on complete acceptance of the fact that in order to have a decent house or education, Blacks must move into a white neighborhood. This reinforces . . . the idea that 'white' is automatically better and 'Black' is by definition inferior."

Stokely Carmichael, chairman of SNCC

November 5, 1968
Richard Nixon wins the presidential election.

1969
To boost African American economic development, the Nixon administration begins affirmative action programs.

March 17, 1972
President Nixon asks Congress to stop all busing of students to desegregate schools.

Activists with the NAACP and other moderate groups disagreed with the direction Black Power was taking the Civil Rights Movement. They knew calls for violence, even in self-defense, would not win public support. Nor did these moderates think Blacks had the financial or political resources to create their own independent institutions. These differences split the Civil Rights Movement just at the moment a new president appeared.

A poster showing four women demonstrating for the release of six members of the Black Panther Party from the Niantic Connecticut State Women's Prison

Credit: Women's Farm in Connecticut, 1969

> "[Black Power] is a reverse Mississippi, a reverse Hitler, a reverse Ku Klux Klan."
>
> **Roy Wilkins**, NAACP executive director, July 5, 1966

A Black Panther convention at the Lincoln Memorial, 1972

Presidential Election of 1968

The nation was bogged down in a deadly war in Vietnam. Martin Luther King Jr. and former U.S. Attorney General Robert Kennedy had been assassinated. Riots shook cities each summer. When Americans went to the polls in November 1968, they wanted to elect a president who would calm things down.

In August, Democrats gathered for their party convention in Chicago. Delegates nominated Vice President Hubert Humphrey (1911–1978), but the process was disastrous. Inside the convention hall, fistfights broke out among delegates.

Outside, things were worse.

Chicago swelled with anti-war protesters. On August 28, as protesters marched toward the convention site, police stopped them with clubs, tear gas, and rifles. The violence caused many voters to reject the Democratic candidate.

BLACK PANTHER PARTY

The Black Panther Party was a militant civil rights group founded in 1966 to combat police brutality in inner cities. Although the party was never large, it gained national attention because of a tragedy on April 6, 1968. Black Panthers Eldridge Cleaver (1935–1998) and 18-year-old Bobby Hutton (1950–1968) ambushed and wounded Oakland, California, police officers. After fleeing to a nearby apartment, the Panthers and police got into a shootout. Cleaver was wounded, so he and Hutton decided to surrender. Hutton removed his shirt so police would know he was unarmed. But when the teen exited the building with his hands up, the police barraged him with bullets. Hutton's death catapulted the Panthers to national fame.

A Vietnam War protest, 1967

Republicans nominated former Vice President Richard Nixon. Although he had a record of supporting civil rights, now Nixon wanted to persuade Southern whites to vote for him. So, he developed the "Southern strategy." Nixon tried to convince Southern whites to back him by stoking their racial prejudices.

During the campaign, Nixon vowed to restore "law and order." One of his aides recorded what Nixon meant by this phrase. "Irish, Ital, Pole, Mex were afraid of Negroes." When these voters heard Nixon promise to restore order, they interpreted it as a pledge to lock up Black people. This kind of phrase is known as a "dog whistle."

WONDER WHY?

Do politicians still use dog whistles? Find speeches by Presidents Bush, Obama, and Trump. What do you notice about each language style? Who is using what phrases to indicate ideals that might be sexist or xenophobic or racist?

> "There can be no progress without order, no freedom without order, no justice without order."
>
> **Richard Nixon, 1968**

Nixon was not the only candidate fueling racial fears. George Wallace from Alabama ran as an independent in 1968. He opposed the Fair Housing Law, claiming it violated property rights. "I feel that whenever a bill is passed which says your grandmother can be put in jail . . . because she refused to sell or lease a house to someone, then the most basic civil right in this country has been destroyed." Wallace ignored how housing discrimination impacted the civil rights of Black people.

The Democratic National Convention in Chicago, August 26, 1968

Credit: Warren K. Leffler, *U.S. News & World Report* magazine collection

Nixon won the election by a razor-thin margin. Although he would make important progress in African American education and employment, his determination to keep the support of conservative whites damaged race relations.

CONNECT

Take a look at a series of maps of the 1968 election results. Based on these maps, how effective was Nixon's Southern strategy?

Richmond elections 1968

The End of School Segregation in the South

Although the U.S. Supreme Court ruled in 1954 that segregated schools were unconstitutional, most Southern Black children still attended all-Black schools in 1968. Then, in May 1968, the Supreme Court ruled in *Green v. School Board of New Kent County* that the South's segregated education systems must be dismantled "root and branch." In response to this decision, Nixon made a political calculation.

Nixon at a campaign rally

Credit: Ollie Atkins, White House photographer

According to the Civil Rights Act of 1964, all federal funding was slashed for schools that refused to obey court-ordered integration. Nixon decided to ignore this rule and let the courts take the lead on integration. Then, white voters would blame the judicial system—not him—when Black students attended their schools. Roy Wilkins, chairman of the NAACP, said Nixon's decision was "Almost enough to make you vomit." The NAACP filed a lawsuit to force the president to enforce the law.

George Wallace addressing an audience at the Democratic National Convention in Atlantic City, New Jersey, August 1964

Credit: Warren K. Leffler, *U.S. News & World Report* magazine collection

Nixon's own racism probably impacted his refusal to support integration. The president considered African Americans uncivilized. He told an aide that they were "basically . . . just out of the trees." In another conversation, Nixon said Mexicans were dishonest, but, "They don't live like a bunch of dogs, which the Negroes do live like."

Finally, after two years of delaying the inevitable, Nixon decided to enforce the court's integration order. But he did so quietly, determined to avoid the violent scenes that had accompanied integration in Little Rock, Arkansas, in 1957.

An integrated classroom in Washington, DC, 1957

Credit: Warren K. Leffler, *U.S. News & World Report* magazine collection

WONDER WHY?

What role do protests play in politics today? Are the protests different from what they were during the Civil Rights Era?

First, Nixon created local advisory boards in seven Southern states. Black and white board members worked out the details of how to integrate their schools. Then, Nixon invited Southern state education committees to the White House, where he dangled both a carrot and a stick in their faces. Legislators were warned that if they resisted integration, Nixon would yank away their federal funding. But, if they peacefully desegregated, he would find extra money for their states.

The strategy worked. Before 1969, only 186,000 Southern Black children out of 3 million attended schools with white children. By the end of 1970, that number rose to 2.6 million.

> "You will be better advised to watch what we do instead of what we say."
>
> **John Mitchell**, aide to President Nixon, to civil rights activists

Northern Schools Remain Segregated

Northern schools were also segregated. Not because of Jim Crow laws but because Black and white children lived in different neighborhoods. Although the cause was different, the result was the same. Suburban schools that served white students received far more resources than the urban schools that Black children attended.

This divide was clearly visible in New York City in early 1960s. Many white families moved to the suburbs, so schools in white neighborhoods were half empty. In contrast, Black and Latino schools were so crowded that students had to attend in four-hour shifts. In 1964, 460,000 Black and Latino students walked out in protest. In response, the district proposed a school pairing plan to bus transfer students between Black and Latino schools and white schools.

The backlash was swift. In March 1964, 15,000 white parents borrowed a tactic from the Civil Rights Movement and staged a protest march. They called their group the "Parents and Taxpayers" and carried signs that read, "Keep our children in neighborhood schools."

Although race was not mentioned, it was clear that these parents wanted to keep their children in all-white schools in their all-white neighborhoods. This pattern repeated itself across the country when busing was used to integrate.

CONNECT

After 1968, corporations such as McDonalds recruited Black businessmen to purchase restaurants in city centers and encouraged them to hire Black employees. Read an article about McDonalds and watch a commercial produced in the 1990s to persuade Black youth to work at McDonalds. What hidden messages about inner-city culture are evident in this ad?

NPR codeswitch McDonalds Black

In 1972, President Nixon ran for reelection. Once again, he was competing against George Wallace, a fierce opponent of busing. In March, after Wallace's support among white voters rose, Nixon gave a televised speech and proposed Congress halt all integration busing. This pleased conservative whites.

But Nixon also said Congress should pass a law to "establish reasonable national standards" so children of all races everywhere could receive a quality education. This appealed to moderate whites and African Americans. Every civil rights decision Nixon made was with an eye to his political future.

The 1974 U.S. Supreme Court decision *Milliken v. Bradley* signaled a slowdown on desegregation in Northern schools. Conservative justices ruled that segregated schools were legal if they were the result of where people chose to live and not a deliberate strategy by government to separate Black and white children. So, as more whites moved to the suburbs, schools in cities such as Detroit, Michigan, and Milwaukee, Wisconsin, became highly segregated. They remain so today.

Black Capitalism

Black capitalism was Nixon's solution for helping African Americans economically. Nixon linked Black capitalism to Black Power. He promised that when African Americans owned their own businesses and homes, they would gain "Black pride, Black jobs, Black opportunity, and, yes, Black Power." Nixon believed tax breaks and loans were better than handouts.

The president established the Office of Minority Business Enterprise (OMBE) in 1969. This agency recruited and advised minority-owned businesses. During Nixon's presidency, the value of products purchased from minority-owned businesses increased by 265 percent.

> "Nixon was an almost completely political animal . . . he made decisions based on how they affected him politically, not based on whether they were right or wrong."
>
> **James Farmer**, civil rights activist

The Philadelphia Plan was another part of Black capitalism. This affirmative action program focused on the cities of Philadelphia, Pennsylvania; San Francisco, California; St. Louis, Missouri; and Cleveland, Ohio. Affirmative action refers to proactive steps companies take to increase the number of minorities they hire.

Implemented in 1969, the Philadelphia Plan banned discrimination in companies and labor unions with federal contracts. The plan also set goals for the number of minorities these companies must hire. Initially, the program applied only to construction companies with federal contracts of more than $500,000. However, in 1970, Nixon extended the program to businesses with federal contracts of at least $50,000.

Black Lives Matter protestors in Minnesota, 2015

Credit: Fibonacci Blue (CC BY 2.0)

Nixon viewed this program as a hand up, not a handout. Affirmative action opponents sued over the Philadelphia Plan, calling it reverse racism.

However, the U.S. Supreme Court upheld it. Justice Harry Blackmun (1908–1999) wrote, "In order to get beyond racism, we must first take account of race. There is no other way."

Nixon has a muddled civil rights legacy. His refusal to enforce busing meant segregation increased in Northern schools. However, he oversaw the desegregation of Southern classrooms.

Privately, Nixon spoke scornfully about African Americans, but he also funded Black businesses to help strengthen the economies in Black neighborhoods. Do you think one outweighs the other?

AN APPALLED PRESIDENT

After Nixon took office in 1969, a study revealed how little money the federal government gave to Black colleges. Of the $4 billion spent on higher education in 1969, only $119 million went to historically Black schools. Robert Brown, special assistant to Nixon, said, "This represented only 3 percent, and the president was appalled." Nixon pledged to change this. During the next decade, government funding for Black colleges rose to $1 billion.

What About Now?

The Civil Rights Movement forced the American political system to change. Activists pressured, shamed, and inspired leaders to expand racial equality. But, despite major improvements, racial inequality and injustice persist.

Are we in the midst of a twenty-first century Civil Rights Movement? The NAACP still lobbies Congress for reforms. Movements such as Black Lives Matter use social media to organize protests and marches against racial wrongs.

During the summer of 2020, after the death of George Floyd at the hands of the police, there seemed to be growing awareness of the need for reform at all levels of society to combat institutional racism.

America will not achieve racial equality until its political leaders are willing to embrace civil rights as a moral issue. Political leadership during the twentieth century Civil Rights Movement transformed the nation. A similar revolution could happen again, but only if citizens demand it. As the history of the Civil Rights Movement demonstrates, when the people lead, the leaders will follow.

WONDER WHY?

What do you think are the next steps toward racial equality that American society needs to take?

PROJECT

Dog Whistle Dictionary

Today, politicians often speak in coded words or phrases. These dog whistles contain hidden meanings that appeal to racial biases of certain listeners. For example, the phrase "illegal alien" does not describe a specific racial or ethnic group. But, for some people, this phrase evokes a fear of Mexican immigrants crossing the Southern border. Citizens need to recognize dog whistles so they know when a politician is manipulating their emotions.

- **Research political dog whistles used in the last election campaign.**
- **Create a dog whistle dictionary.** Include the real definition of each word/phrase and its hidden meaning.
- **Reflect on how dog whistles can negatively affect race relations.** How is this especially true in an election year.

Word Power!

What vocabulary words did you discover? Can you figure out the meanings of these words? Look in the glossary for help!

affirmative action, busing, capitalism, dog whistle, minority, moral, oppressed, sexist, prejudice, and reverse racism

TEXT TO WORLD

Do you see a new Civil Rights Movement starting? Do you choose to be a part of it? Why or why not?

PROJECT

Ten Point Program for Today

In 1966, the Black Panther Party wrote its goals for African Americans in a statement called the Ten Point Program. Evaluate your community and make goals for your future.

- **Make a list of what you think are the biggest problems in your home, school, community, and country today.**
- **Share your list of problems with some peers.** Work together to come up with a Ten Point Program for twenty-first-century America.
- **How does your program compare with that of the Black Panthers?**
- **Go to the websites of the Republican and Democratic candidates for president in 2020.** Which of the needs on your Ten Point Program do these candidates address?

Go to this link to view the platform of the Black Panther Party. What did this group consider the most pressing problems facing African Americans?

DPLA Black Power movement

2020 INEQUALITY STATS

Young Black men are 21 times more likely than young white men to be shot by police.

Blacks are imprisoned six times more often than whites.

Forty-two percent of Black children are educated in high-poverty schools.

Black family income is two-thirds that of white families.

The Black unemployment rate is twice that of whites.

Only 40 percent of African Americans own a home compared to 70 percent of whites.

In 2019, there were only three African American members of the U.S. Senate and no Black governors.

abolish: to completely put an end to something.

activist: someone who works to bring about political or social change.

adjourn: to temporarily end a meeting.

affirmative action: an active effort to improve the employment or educational opportunities of members of minority groups.

alienate: to cause someone to feel isolated.

alliance: a group of people who join together and agree to help each other.

amendment: an article added to the U.S. Constitution.

annotate: to add descriptions or notes.

assassinate: to murder an important person for political or religious reasons.

attorney general: the head of the U.S. Department of Justice.

backlash: a strong negative reaction by a lot of people to a political or social change.

ban: to legally prohibit something.

bias: prejudice in favor or against something or someone.

bigotry: intolerance toward someone who looks or thinks differently than oneself.

Black Lives Matter: a protest movement founded to defeat white supremacy and build local power to intervene in violence inflicted on Black communities by the state and individuals.

boycott: to refuse to buy certain goods or use certain services as a form of protest.

brutality: great physical and mental cruelty.

busing: the practice of assigning and transporting students to schools within a school district in order to racially integrate schools.

cabinet: the senior advisers to the executive branch of government, headed by the president.

calculation: an assessment of risks and possibilities.

capitalism: an economy in which people, not the government, own the factories, ships, and land used in the production and distribution of goods.

citizen: a person who has all the rights and responsibilities that come with being a full member of a country.

civil rights: the basic rights that all citizens of a society are supposed to have, such as the right to vote.

Civil Rights Movement: a national movement for racial equality in the 1950s and 1960s.

cloture: a procedure used by a legislature to end a debate and taking a vote.

commerce: buying and selling goods on a large scale.

commission: a group of people officially given a particular task to complete.

confrontational: tending to deal with situations in an aggressive way.

consensual: when all parties agree.

conservative: holding on to traditional values and being reluctant to make political or religious changes.

constitution: the basic principles and laws of a nation or state that determine the powers and duties of the government and guarantees certain rights to the people in it.

corrupt: behaving dishonestly for money or personal gain.

criteria: the standard by which something is judged or measured.

defiance: bold disobedience.

delegate: a person authorized to represent others, especially at a conference or political assembly.

deliberate: to do something consciously and intentionally.

deploy: to move troops into position for military action.

deprive: to deny someone the possession or use of something.

desegregate: to end segregation.

destiny: something that was bound to happen.

discrimination: the unjust treatment of specific groups of people.

dismantle: to take something apart.

diversity: including people from different races, cultures, genders, sexual preferences, and other identities.

doctrine: a set of beliefs.

dog whistle: a subtle political message aimed at a particular group and often recognized only by members of this group.

drone: a low continuous sound.

economic: relating to the production, distribution, and consumption of goods and services.

embalm: to treat a dead body with chemicals to prevent it from rotting.

equality: being the same in power and status.

escalate: to become more serious.

ethnic: a social group that shares a common culture, religion, or language.

evict: to kick someone out of a property.

exclude: to deny someone access.

executive branch: the branch of the government charged with enforcing the law.

expel: to drive or push out.

federal: relating to the central government rather than the states.

felony: a serious crime.

filibuster: a political procedure where one or more members of the U.S. Congress debate over a proposed bill in order to delay or entirely prevent the bill from being voted on.

foundation: an underlying idea or principle.

gerrymander: to divide a state or county into election districts in a way that favors one political party.

ghetto: a section of a city, often rundown, in which members of a minority group live because of social, legal, or economic pressure.

harassment: aggressive pressure or intimidation.

heckle: to tease and taunt.

immigration: coming to live permanently in a foreign country.

implement: to put a plan into effect.

implicate: to show that someone is involved in wrongdoing.

inequality: differences in opportunity and treatment based on social, ethnic, racial, or economic qualities.

inferior: lower in rank or status or quality.

infrastructure: basic facilities such as roads, power plants, and communication systems.

inherently: in an essential or characteristic way.

injustice: unfair action or treatment.

institution: an established law, practice, or custom.

institutional racism: a pattern of social institutions such as government or schools giving negative treatment to a group of people based on race.

insurrection: a violent uprising against the government.

integrate: desegregating, or bringing Black people and white people together in schools, workplaces, and neighborhoods.

integrated: including members of different races, religions, and backgrounds.

interpret: to explain or understand the deep meaning of something.

interstate: between two states.

intimidation: to frighten or threaten someone.

Jim Crow: the legally enforced discrimination of Black people that led to the practice of segregating African Americans in the United States.

justice: fair treatment.

Ku Klux Klan (KKK): a terrorist group formed after the Civil War that believes white Christians should hold the power in society.

legacy: something handed down from the past that has a long-lasting impact.

legislation: the act of making new laws.

liberal: willing to discard traditional values or practices and open to new ideas.

literacy: the ability to read and write.

lobby: to seek to influence politicians about a particular issue.

loot: to steal goods, typically during a riot.

lynching: when a mob, without any legal authority or authorization, kills someone.

manifesto: a public declaration of goals.

martyr: someone who dies for a cause.

migrate: to move from one place to another.

militant: combative and aggressive in support of a political or social cause.

militia: a group of citizens who are trained to fight but who serve only in time of emergency.

minority: a group of people who differ from the main group in race, gender, language, religion, or other differences. Minorities are often discriminated against.

minstrel: white entertainers who blackened their faces and performed songs and dances.

moderate: a person whose political views are not extreme or intense.

monitor: to oversee.

moral: ethical and honest behavior.

morality: beliefs about right and wrong.

mortgage: a loan from a bank, usually to purchase a house.

nation-state: a self-governed political territory where people share the same culture.

neutral: not favoring one side over another.

nominate: to formally propose a candidate for election.

nonviolent: characterized by not using physical force or power.

obstacle: something that block's the way and slows progress.

open housing: the opportunity to purchase or rent housing without being discriminated against.

oppress: to use unjust or cruel authority and power to persecute someone.

origin: where a person comes from.

oversight: to watch over and manage something carefully.

petition: a written appeal to government.

pistol whip: to hit or beat someone with a pistol.

platform: the declared policies of a political party.

poll tax: a tax required as a qualification for voting.

prejudice: a negative opinion formed without knowledge or evidence against people from a specific group.

prelude: an early part.

primary source: a firsthand account of a topic from people who had a direct connection to it.

priority: a thing that is regarded as more important than something else.

prosecute: to try to prove in a court of law that someone is guilty of committing a crime.

provoke: to arouse anger in someone.

pummel: to pound or beat someone.

quell: to stop or reduce.

race: a group of people of common ancestry who share certain physical characteristics such as skin color.

racism: negative opinions or treatment of people based on race and the notion that people of a different race are inferior because of their race.

racist: hatred of people of a different race.

rape: sexual intercourse without consent.

ratify: to give official approval of something, such as a constitutional amendment.

Reconstruction: the era following the U.S. Civil War when the federal government tried to reunify the country and integrate African Americans into society.

redline: to refuse a loan or insurance to someone because they live in an area of town considered a risky investment.

refinance: to replace an existing loan with a new one with lower interest rates.

refrain: to stop oneself from doing something.

register: the requirement for citizens to prove eligibility to an official prior to voting.

residency: the fact of living in a place.

reverse racism: a problematic term describing discrimination on the basis of race directed against a member of a privileged racial group, often used as a criticism of programs that address racial inequality.

riot: a gathering of people that gets out of control and violent.

segregation: the enforced separation of different racial groups in a community or country.

segregationist: a person who supports the policy of enforced separation of different racial groups.

self-sufficiency: being able to supply one's own needs without outside assistance.

sit-in: a form of protest in which people occupy a space and refuse to move.

slum: a crowded area of a city where poor people live and buildings are in bad condition.

slur: an insulting comment.

strategy: a plan of action to achieve a goal.

stunted: prevented from developing properly.

sundown town: a community that used laws, violence, and intimidation to prevent non-whites from living there.

suppression: preventing something from happening.

tenant farmer: a person who farms rented land.

tenement: a rundown, overcrowded apartment in a poor section of the city.

trumped-up: false or made up, as in an accusation.

unanimous: having the agreement of everyone.

unconstitutional: not in agreement or accordance with a political constitution, especially the U.S. Constitution.

undaunted: not intimidated or discouraged by difficulty, danger, or disappointment.

unemployment: joblessness.

uphold: to support a decision that has already been made.

violate: to fail to obey or follow the rules of a law.

white supremacy: the racist belief that white people are superior to those of all other races and should therefore dominate society.

xenophobia: an intense or irrational dislike or fear of people from other countries.

BOOKS

Brimner, Larry Dane. *Twelve Days in May: Freedom Rides 1961*. Calkins Creek, 2017.

Burgan, Michael. *The Voting Rights Act of 1965: An Interactive History Adventure*. Capstone Press, 2015.

Lowery, Lynda Blackmon. *Turning 15 on the Road to Freedom: My Story of the 1965 Selma Voting Rights March*. Penguin, 2015.

Schwartz, Heather E. *Locked Up for Freedom: Civil Rights Protesters at the Leesburg Stockade*. Millbrook Press, 2017.

WEBSITES

National Civil Rights Museum at the Lorraine Motel: civilrightsmuseum.org

African American Odyssey: lcweb2.loc.gov/ammem/aaohtml/exhibit

Voices of the Civil Rights Movement: loc.gov/exhibits/civilrights

We Shall Overcome—Historic Places of the Civil Rights Movement: nps.gov/nr/travel/civilrights

QR CODE GLOSSARY

PAGE 6: arcgis.com/apps/MapJournal/index.html?appid=56186312471f47eca8aff16a8a990aa8

PAGE 11: projects.propublica.org/miseducation

PAGE 24: history.com/news/the-story-behind-the-famous-little-rock-nine-scream-image

PAGE 25: kqed.org/lowdown/30098/why-have-americas-public-schools-gotten-more-racially-segregated

PAGE 38: loc.gov/exhibits/civil-rights-act/multimedia/kennedys-civil-rights-address.html

PAGE 42: al.com/living/2014/02/young_man_attacked_by_german_s.html

PAGE 42: crdl.usg.edu/cgi/crdl?dbs=crdl&ini=crdl.ini&query=Names_phrase:%22Gadsden%2C+Walter%22

PAGE 42: readingthepictures.org/2013/01/on-the-wrong-side-of-history-further-thoughts-on-an-iconic-civil-rights-photograph

PAGE 43: senate.gov/artandhistory/history/common/generic/CivilRightsAct1964.htm

PAGE 43: kids-clerk.house.gov/middle-school/lesson.html?intID=17

PAGE 46: thirteen.org/wnet/jimcrow/voting_start.html

PAGE 47: amsterdamnews.com/news/2020/jan/30/americas-first-black-vote

PAGE 49: gilderlehrman.org/sites/default/files/content-images/09090p1.jpg

PAGE 53: youtube.com/watch?v=Bnmc_8pA1tY

PAGE 57: everydayarcade.com/games/the-voter-suppression-trail

PAGE 58: youtube.com/watch?v=ieB3ukWB3tQ

PAGE 62: youtube.com/watch?v=PE9jA1dU3jE

QR CODE GLOSSARY (CONTINUED)

PAGE 63: sundown.tougaloo.edu/content.php?file=sundowntowns-whitemap.html

PAGE 65: loc.gov/exhibits/civil-rights-act/multimedia/white-backlash-in-the-north.html

PAGE 68: washingtonpost.com/graphics/2018/national/segregation-us-cities

PAGE 73: youtube.com/watch?v=jJgN6BWiCfQ

PAGE 79: people.howstuffworks.com/jane-elliott.htm

PAGE 88: dsl.richmond.edu/voting/indelections.php?year=1968

PAGE 93: npr.org/sections/codeswitch/2020/02/04/398793395/when-mcdonalds-was-a-road-to-black-liberation

PAGE 97: dp.la/primary-source-sets/the-black-power-movement/sources/388

SELECTED BIBLIOGRAPHY

Bash, Dana. "Following John Lewis on Civil Rights Journey 'Touched by the Spirit of History'," *CNN Politics*. CNN, 9 March 2018. Web. 10 March 2020. cnn.com/2018/03/07/politics/john-lewis-bloody-sunday-anniversary-reporters-notebook/index.html.

Brown, DaNeen. "The Determined Father Who Took Linda Brown by the Hand and Made History." *The Washington Post*. Washington Post Co., 27 Mar. 2018. Web. 12 Apr. 2020. washingtonpost.com/news/retropolis/wp/2018/03/27/the-determined-black-dad-who-took-linda-brown-by-the-hand-and-stepped-into-history.

"Brown v. Board: Timeline of School Integration in the U.S." *Teaching Tolerance*. Southern Poverty Law Center, Spring 2004. Web. 6 Apr. 2020. tolerance.org/magazine/spring-2004/brown-v-board-timeline-of-school-integration-in-the-us.

Hall, Simon. "The NAACP, Black Power, and the African American Freedom Struggle, 1966–1969." *The Historian*. 28 Feb. 2007. Web. 13 Apr. 2020. onlinelibrary.wiley.com/doi/full/10.1111/j.1540-6563.2007.00174.x.

Menand, Louis. "The Color of Law: Voting Rights and the Southern Way of Life." *The New Yorker*. 1 July 2013. newyorker.com/magazine/2013/07/08/the-color-of-law.

"Meredith March." SNCC Digital. Duke University. N.d. Web. 27 Mar. 2020. snccdigital.org/events/meredith-march.

"Report of the National Advisory Commission on Civil Disorders." Eisenhower Commission. 1968. Web. 22 Mar. 2020. eisenhowerfoundation.org/docs/kerner.pdf.

Skrentny, John D. "Zigs and Zags: Richard Nixon and the New Politics of Race." *Winning While Losing: Civil Rights, the Conservative Movement, and the Presidency from Nixon to Obama*.

Worthington, Marianne. "The Campaign Rhetoric of George Wallace in the 1968 Presidential Election." *The Upsilonian*. University of the Cumberlands, 1992. Web. 29 Mar. 2020.